DIRK TIM

Valletta

A PERSONAL CITY GUIDE

DAMON ALLEN
VERONICA BARBARA
JENNIFER ROSE BUGEJA
NARCY CALAMATTA
INGRID EOMOIS
DANE MUNRO
PAUL SPITERI
VINCE ZAMMIT

EDITED BY
MARTIN BUGELLI

midsea BOOKS

Valletta A PERSONAL CITY GUIDE

Published by Midsea Books Ltd,
68, Carmelites Street,
68, Sta Venera SVR1724, Malta
www.midseabooks.com

Edited by Martin Bugelli

First published in 2018
All rights reserved

Editorial Copyright © Midsea Books, 2018
Literary Copyright © the authors, 2018
Photo Copyright © the photographers,
as per Photo Credits

Map Copyright © Midsea Books, 2018
All rights reserved. No part of this publication may be reproduced in any form or by any means, without the permission of the rightful owners.

Produced by Midsea Books

ISBN: 978-99932-7-668-5

PHOTO CREDITS
AB, 172; CH, 143, CP, 171; DOI/RP, 1; Google Maps, 2, 3; GF, 53; HM, 49; HM/EDW, 46[t]; MA, 181[b]; MB, 6, 7, 15, 26, 29, 33, 36, 37, 42, 43, 46, 52, 54, 55, 60, 61, 62, 65, 69, 73, 75, 78, 80, 82, 85, 89, 90, 93, 97, 98, 100, 106, 107, 110, 111, 113, 114, 125, 131, 166, 169, 174, 190, 192, backcover and flap; MB/JPB, 8, 16, 104, 128; MB/SJCCF, 135, 136, MB/SJCCF/JPB, 126, 129, 132, 134, 146, 149, 150, 151, 152, 154, 159; NB, 63; PA/DR, 147; PC, 70; SP, 167; TF, 173; TM, 115, 116, 118, 121, 122; UP, 168, 170; V18, 38; VM, cover, 4, 9, 10, 11, 18[t], 25, 28, 35, 57, 67, 108, 112, 138, 142, 148, 163, 164, 180, 185; VM/AB, 21, 31, 58; VM/BLC, 13; VM/CV, 12; VM/CW, 145; VM/GI, 44, 187, 188; VM/HM, 47, 48; VM/HM/CW, 47; VM/IN, 182; VM/IM, 22; VM/JS, 44, 59, 102; VM/MG, 177; VM/MW, 56, 140, VM/PV, 18[b], 94

PHOTOGRAPHERS: Joe P. Borg (JPB); Aaron Briffa (AB); Martin Bugelli (MA); Geo Fürst (GF); Mario Galea (MG); Gregory Iron Photography (GI); Iven Maniscalco (IM); Ilena Navarro (IN); Photocity (PC); Reuben Piscopo (RP); Dragana Rankovic (DR); Jürgen Scicluna (JS); Peter Vanicsek (PV); Clive Vella (CV); Mike Watson Photography (MW); Chen Weizhong (CW); Etan Doyle White (EDW)

INSTITUTIONS/AGENCIES: Associated British Picture Corporation (AB); Birgu Local Council (BLC); Chevron.co.uk (CH); Columbia Pictures (CP); Department of Information (DOI); Heritage Malta (HM); Malta Tourism Authority (MTA); Midsea Books Photo Archive (MB); Nenu The Baker (NB); Panda.com.mt (PA); St John's Co-Cathedral Foundation (SJCCF); Sony Pictures (SP); Teatru Manoel (TM); Twentieth Century Fox (TF); Universal Pictures (UP); Valletta 2018 (V18); ViewingMalta.com (VM)

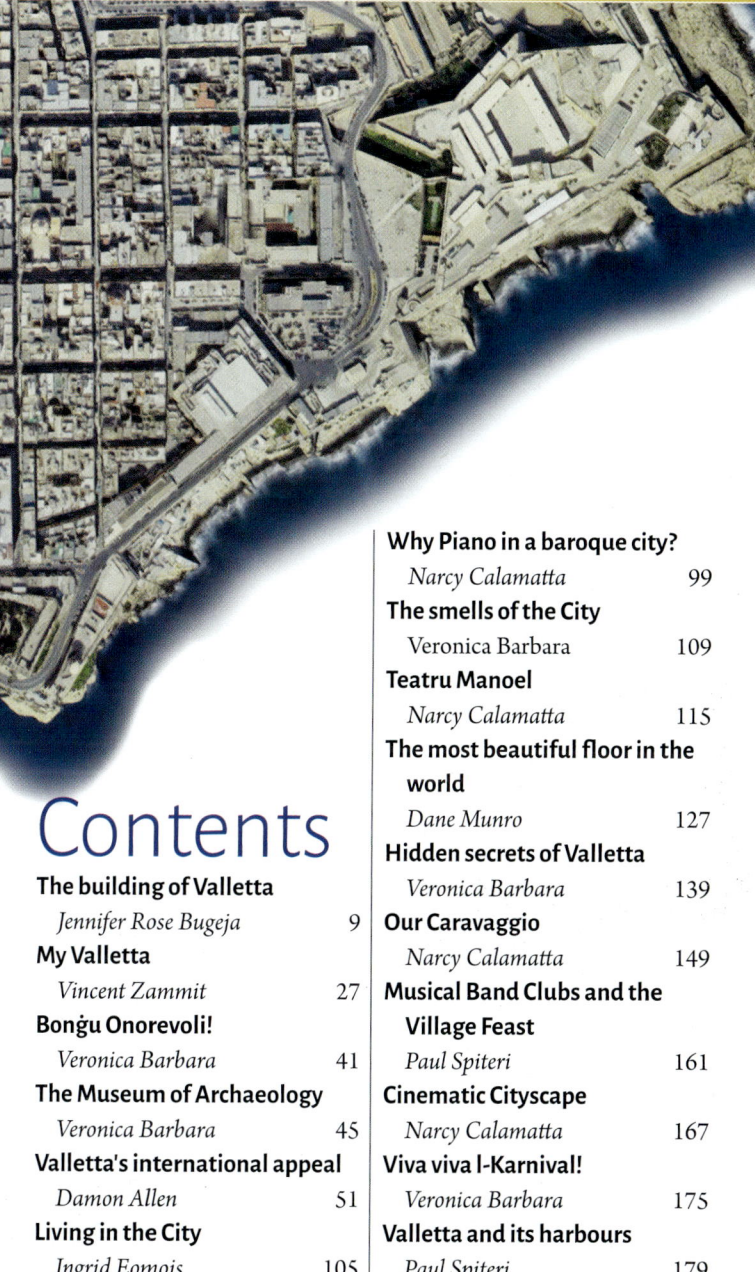

Contents

The building of Valletta
Jennifer Rose Bugeja   9

My Valletta
Vincent Zammit   27

Bonġu Onorevoli!
Veronica Barbara   41

The Museum of Archaeology
Veronica Barbara   45

Valletta's international appeal
Damon Allen   51

Living in the City
Ingrid Eomois   105

Why Piano in a baroque city?
Narcy Calamatta   99

The smells of the City
Veronica Barbara   109

Teatru Manoel
Narcy Calamatta   115

The most beautiful floor in the world
Dane Munro   127

Hidden secrets of Valletta
Veronica Barbara   139

Our Caravaggio
Narcy Calamatta   149

Musical Band Clubs and the Village Feast
Paul Spiteri   161

Cinematic Cityscape
Narcy Calamatta   167

Viva viva l-Karnival!
Veronica Barbara   175

Valletta and its harbours
Paul Spiteri   179

Valletta **A PERSONAL CITY GUIDE**

Crowds throng Valletta during *Notte Bianca*

A personal introduction
DIRK TIMMERMAN

My passion for Malta was born after I started visiting the island in 2002, after having read an article about Madonna and Guy Ritchie filming the romantic comedy remake Swept Away *in autumn 2001. As many recurrent visitors afterwards state – I immediately fell in love with the Island. 2002 was a time when the internet was just a few years old, and when the old English buses were still on the roads, driving tourists to the many beautiful places on the Island.*

Malta has always been a country in full development. As a Belgian citizen, I was always surprised how they changed things in the country and how the number of tourists has grown so much during the last decade. If you compare the Blue Lagoon in Comino today, with how it was 16 years ago for instance, you will see the big difference in the number of tourists who have found their way to this beautiful island to have a dive. Gozo has also certainly achieved celebrity status right now, with the collapse of the Azure Window in March 2017. This tourist attraction, which had served as the backdrop to the marriage of Daenerys Targaryen and Khal Drogo in the HBO series, Game of Thrones, became an even bigger attraction after its disappearance!

Malta is without a doubt the most promising island in the Mediterranean, with this needing to be confirmed during 2018, when Valletta is, together with the Dutch city Leeuwarden, the European Capital of Culture. If you plan to visit Malta, and more specifically, its capital city Valletta, this book is meant to be the best companion for you to understand this unique country.

Why? It is not the classic, run-of-the-mill, tourist guide of the type you'll find everywhere, but more of a story-telling experience prepared by

Valletta A PERSONAL CITY GUIDE

eight of the best tourist guides in Malta. This idea hatched in my mind in September 2016, when I thought of publishing a book prepared by local tourist guides, an idea that apparently had not been dealt with before. I contacted a whole range of tourist guides and I received so much response, that I had to select eight fantastic tourist guides out of all the candidates.

I asked them all to submit two or three essays about their favourite subjects in Malta, and to my great surprise there was no overlap and all the works blended very well. This is now this book. The eight Maltese tourist guides chose the subject-matter themselves, based on their knowledge and experience with visitors, making this book the best special guide for the Maltese Islands that you could have.

With the trust placed in me by the eight guides who collaborated on this project, I then went on to find the appropriate book publisher. This proved to be easy, as Joseph Mizzi from Midsea Books immediately made me sure that he was the right man to publish this book. It goes without saying I am very grateful to the Maltese guides and to Joseph Mizzi and his team at Midsea Books.

I hope you enjoy reading this book as much as we enjoyed preparing it for you …

… with a passion for Malta.

Street performers

Lower Barrakka and the Old Customs House

Valletta A PERSONAL CITY GUIDE

Entrance to the Grand Master's Palace

The building of Valletta

JENNIFER ROSE BUGEJA

Origins of the Knights of St John
Just before the end of the 11th century, a group of devout merchants from Amalfi were granted a piece of land close to the Holy Sepulchre in Jerusalem, where they established or restored a monastery that was administered by Italian Benedictines. These monks set up a hospice, dedicated to St John the Baptist, providing support and medical assistance to poor and sick pilgrims who visited the Holy Land.

Valletta **A PERSONAL CITY GUIDE**

In Guardia re-enactments

After the success of the First Crusade in 1099, the Christian armies entered Jerusalem and found this monastery to be a well-organised hospital, being managed by a certain Brother Gerard. In due course, the hospital earned recognition as an autonomous entity, and received numerous gifts and donations. In fact, by 1113, Pope Pascal II had sanctioned a Papal Bull (*Pie Apostolato Voluntatis*) stating that the brotherhood running this hospital would be provided with papal protection and with the right to elect its superiors. Eventually, it was declared a self-governing Order, when the Pope issued a jurisdictional exemption from the Patriarch of Jerusalem. Several documents refer to Brother Gerard as being the founder and the administrator of what in time became known as, the 'Knights Hospitallers', a title that undoubtedly characterised their mission. They were also referred to as the Knights of St John, in view of their patron saint, St John the Baptist.

THE BUILDING OF VALLETTA

Over subsequent decades, the Order continued to thrive, achieving wealth, status and power. Besides their original mission to guard and nurse sick pilgrims, the Order began progressively to broaden its areas of influence. By the mid-12th century, it had also taken up military responsibilities, assimilating within their being, two important missions: the monastic and the military. This meant that, besides the traditional vows of chastity, poverty and obedience, they had become warrior-monks safeguarding Christian possessions against Muslim forces. For the next two centuries, the Order played a significant role in protecting strategic places in the Kingdom of Jerusalem, participating in military expeditions against the Muslims, while also upholding their hospitaller duties.

Historical re-enactment with Grand Master

When, in 1291, the Muslim armies pushed on to take Acre, the last remaining Christian possession in the Holy Land, the Knights of St John decided to set

Valletta seen from Sliema front

Valletta A PERSONAL CITY GUIDE

a temporary base in Limassol, Cyprus. Almost two decades later, they completed the capture of Rhodes, situated in the Aegean Sea, and decided to relocate their headquarters to the City of Rhodes. Being stranded on a small island limited their military endeavours, therefore they had to adapt to new roles. As a result, they constructed a powerful fleet and trained themselves in the art of naval warfare. Rhodes developed into an important piracy hub, controlling hundreds of miles of the Anatolian coastline. Here they became the principal protectors of Christendom withstanding the constant attacks of the Turkish Ottoman Empire, while constantly harassing their ships. However, the Turks put a halt to all this in 1522, when the legendary Turkish Sultan, Süleyman the Magnificent, laid siege to and captured Rhodes, and kicked the Knights out. After two hundred years living on Rhodes, the Knights of St John were compelled to surrender and leave with military honours.

Malta: A problematic start

'*Rien n'est plus connu que le siège de Malte* - Voltaire' (Nothing is better known than the Siege of Malta)

The Order ended up homeless, wondering around Europe in a frantic search for a new base. After lengthy and complicated negotiations, on 24 March 1530, they signed a donation deed that was granted by the Spanish Emperor, Charles V. The Spanish Crown donated the Maltese Islands, together with the North African fort of Tripoli, as a perpetual fief, binding the Order to pay a falcon every year as rent, on All Saints' Day. Besides that, the deed granted the Order full autonomy to maintain their own statutes and adhere to their historic task of pursuing war against the Muslim forces. The Knights set sail from Sicily, and

Falconeering during a re-enactment

THE BUILDING OF VALLETTA

landed in Malta in the autumn of 1530. Having by now established themselves as a maritime force, they were not willing to settle in the inland capital city of Mdina, referred to in Italian as *Citta' Notabile*. Instead, they chose the then fishing town of *Il Borgo*, (now *Birgu* or Vittoriosa), located on one of the peninsulas jutting out in Grand Harbour. Grand Master Philippe Villiers de L'Isle-Adam set up his base at the tip of this promontory, in an old castle known as the *Castrum Maris* (now Fort St Angelo). He immediately started improving and strengthening the castle, but works on other fortifications were slow, possibly indicating that the Knights considered Malta as a temporary base, and still yearned to retake Rhodes.

They still regarded the Maltese Islands as a virtual military, political and economic liability. Yet, despite all the shortcomings, Malta had other advantages, such as the two spacious natural harbours (the Grand Harbour and Marsamxett Harbour) capable of offering safe anchorage to the Order's fleet. Separating these harbours there was a tongue of rocky wasteland, known as Mount Sceberras. The highest point of this promontory was just over fifty metres above sea level, and at its outernmost point, there were a small watchtower and a

Fort St Angelo

chapel, dedicated to St Elmo, the protector of navigators.

In 1541, Antonio Ferramolino, a respectable military engineer from Bergamo, suggested building a strong fortress-city on this headland. He insisted that this was the only feasible solution to defend the islands and to offer shelter to locals in case of an Ottoman invasion. However, Grand Master Juan d'Omedes shot down this idea. For several years, the Knights viewed this venture as too expensive, and one that would take a long time to accomplish. Instead, they decided to build two forts – one located at the head of Mount Sceberras and another one on St Julian's Hill (now *Isla* or Senglea), the peninsula parallel to the Birgu one. Priority was given to the fort constructed on the Sceberras peninsula, as this would defend the entrance to both harbours at the same time. This was named Fort St Elmo and incorporated the old chapel of St Elmo. The fort on St Julian's Hill was named Fort St Michael.

Things took a different turn with the election of the French Grand Master, Jean de Valette, in August of 1557. In his view, building a new city on high grounds, protecting it by side bastions and a strong land front, would transform the sterile isthmus of Mount Sceberras into an invincible and indispensable fortress-city. Moreover, the new city could provide more space to construct private and public edifices, thus accommodating the requirements of the Order, a function that could not be achieved if they remained in Fort St Angelo. In fact, the fulfilment of this project became one of the most important priorities in the agenda of the new Grand Master. He visited the peninsula on a regular basis, taking measurements and inspecting locations. Consequently, he gave clear instructions to bring to the island a reputable engineer from Montalcino, a certain Marco Antonio Quisani, who was not however the only engineer who came to Malta. In fact, from the 1550s to the early 1660s, several reputable Italian military engineers were called upon to present their proposals for the reinforcement of defences and the building of a fortified city on the Sceberras peninsula. Extensive preliminary work was carried out, during those early years.

THE BUILDING OF VALLETTA

Unfortunately, the shortage of finances, and the constant rumours of an imminent Turkish attack, put on hold the execution of this plan. In fact, a relatively short time afterwards, the eminent Turkish Sultan Süleyman the Magnificent, sent a huge fleet of about 190 vessels, carrying a squadron of 28,000 men. This invasion fleet, news of which had been anticipated by spies, appeared on the horizon on 18 May, 1565. The Knights had a force of around 6,100 combatants which included around 3,000 Maltese irregulars. The Ottomans soon discovered that in order to enter Marsamxett Harbour with their fleet, and anchor it safely there, they needed to neutralise Fort St Elmo. Therefore, they immediately attacked this small fort. After over a month of incessant attacks, the fort finally succumbed, offering the Ottomans the possibility to set their camps on the Sceberras peninsula and to fire their guns across

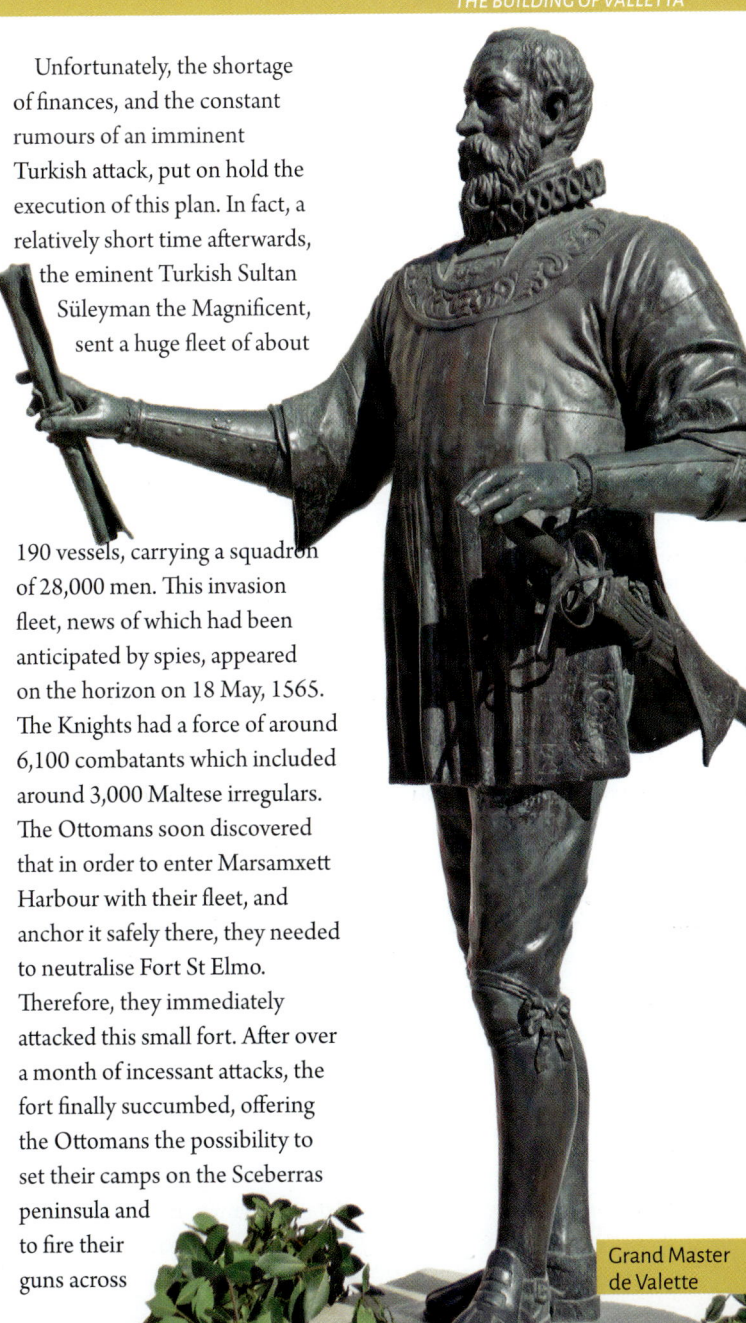

Grand Master de Valette

Valletta **A PERSONAL CITY GUIDE**

the water towards the forts and settlements on the other side, Fort St Angelo, Il Borgo and Fort St Michael. St Elmo's prolonged heroic resistance conceded the Knights ample time to ask for reinforcements, and ignited passion and support in Christian kingdoms throughout Europe. Constant assaults, atrocities and bloodshed continued throughout the summer months. However, the arrival of a large relief force of fresh troops from Spain and Sicily on the 7 September 1565, led the Ottoman armada to withdraw from its siege positions the day after, and sail back to Constantinople in humiliation on the 13 September.

The siege left the island in ruins, with scenes of destruction and devastation especially in the Grand Harbour area. Around two thirds of the inhabitants had lost their lives during fighting or due to illnesses. Together with the famous Siege of Vienna of 1683, the Great Siege of Malta remains one of the most famous sieges of sixteenth and seventeenth century Europe. The victory was a moral boost to a discouraged Christian Europe, since it halted the advance being made by the Ottomans. This siege gave the Knights back their reputation as the epitome of Christian chivalry, and justified their relevance for Christian Europe. This victory also linked the Knights inextricably with Malta, and made them now regard it as their permanent base and home. The Knights immediately realised that they needed to organise an efficient infrastructure programme that included the building of a well-fortified city in

The Great Siege of 1565

order to make sure that their new-found home would not be taken away from them.

Francesco Laparelli: "Give me time and I will give you Life"

Although the siege was over, the Knights were still concerned about what lay ahead. De Valette was convinced that Süleyman would soon launch a fresh attack, probably taking place sometime during spring or summer of 1566. Some leading knights were even considering leaving the island and setting up their headquarters elsewhere, possibly in Syracuse. It was evident that, after four months of incessant bombardments and direct attacks, the fortifications had been devastated and were no longer able to withstand a second Turkish siege. The Grand Master knew that it was important to act at once. Consequently, he decided to reactivate his dream of building a new, fortified city on the Sceberras peninsula.

De Valette immediately dispatched his ambassadors throughout Christian Europe. Besides spreading the news about the victory against the Ottoman Turks, they were instructed to obtain a monetary capital and to persist on asking for troops who would be based on the Island, until the project would be completed. The Knights believed that this was a project too crucial to be entirely delegated to their own engineers so they asked for a reputable military engineer with experience in town planning. Large monetary donations flowed in from all over Europe, while others, such as the Viceroy of Sicily, sent around one thousand stone-cutters, builders and sappers, together with the cash needed to cover their salaries. Likewise, Pope Pius IV provided monetary backing and offered the services of his personal military engineer, Francesco Laparelli. In addition, the Pope promised to grant indulgences to all who donated to this cause.

Francesco Laparelli was from the Italian town of Crotona. In Rome, Laparelli had become an acclaimed military engineer, working for the Pontiff and assisting the famous Michelangelo Buonarroti. Laparelli arrived in Malta on 29 December 1565, and promptly started working on the new project. The arduous task included the demarcation of the site on which the city

Valletta A PERSONAL CITY GUIDE

Great Siege Monument

had to be built, the submission of its plans, together with an effective management plan for its construction. A mere six days after his arrival, he submitted his first proposal to the Grand Master and the Knights' Council, confirming that it was more practical to build a new city on the Sceberras promontory. This first proposal laid the fundamental groundwork for other forthcoming reports, remaining essentially unaltered until the completion of the project. In this report, Laparelli insisted that the restoration and strengthening of existing forts, such as those found at the Borgo and Isola, would be useless if Mount Sceberras remained available to an invading force as they would still be exposed to artillery fire from there. Laparelli also insisted on two important details. The walls of the new city had to incorporate Fort St Elmo, while the land-front had to be built on the highest grounds of the peninsula, some one thousand metres away from Fort St Elmo. This meant that the fortifications would enclose an area three times larger than that of the Borgo.

It was not an easy task persuading a Grand Master who was discouraged by the enormous financial expenditure, and torn between the different viewpoints that were constantly being brought forward. As the Grand Master and his Knights deliberated the proposals submitted by Laparelli, King Phillip II of Spain decided to send another expert, Fra Gabrio Serbelloni. Serbelloni happened to know Laparelli and had previously collaborated with him when working at the Vatican. After visiting the sites and examining Laparelli's maps, he suggested some minor alternations and approved the scheme. The Grand Master immediately assembled the Council and, unanimously, they voted in favour of Laparelli's designs. Laparelli leapt into action. He went on site, ordered the removal of a rubble wall and with its stones he plotted the contour of the city's land front. Preparations were also carried out for the laying of the foundation stone, scheduled to take place six months after the end of the Great Siege.

St Barbara bastion and the Grand Harbour

Valletta A PERSONAL CITY GUIDE

Valletta is born: 28 March 1566

The first stone of the city was laid on Thursday, 28 March 1566. On that day, early in the morning, Grand Master de Valette, in the presence of the local bishop, knights, several church dignitaries, the local nobility and a large Maltese crowd, left the old city of *Il Borgo* and walked in solemn procession all the way to Mount Sceberras. A Holy Inauguration Mass was celebrated at the pinnacle of the peninsula, possibly on the same spot where the Church of Our Lady of Victory would be erected. A huge tent and a provisional, ornamental altar were set up for this special occasion. The rest of the peninsula was festooned with flags showing the coat of arms of the Grand Master, and the emblem of the Order.

Amidst the great rejoicing of the locals and the firing of artillery, just after eleven o'clock in the morning, the symbolic foundation stone was laid in its location. Beneath this stone, the knights decided to place a casket containing gold, silver and bronze coins and some commemorative medals that had been cast exclusively for this event. The bronze coins had the effigy of de Valette on one side whereas on the other side there were different designs, probably five in all. The new city was christened Valletta after its founder. However, in 1567, the Knights added the title, 'most humble', hence the city became known as *Humilissima Civitas Vallettae*. The coat of arms of de Valette, a golden lion on a red shield, was also chosen as the city's emblem.

Works in Progress

The Knights now concentrated all their energies upon the fortifications of the new city. In case of another invasion, the new defences would offer the necessary shelter to its occupants and also to other people from all over the island. They first needed to rebuild Fort St Elmo in a strengthened and enlarged form, with wider ditches, higher spurs and new barracks, furnaces and reservoirs. The fort was incorporated within the city walls.

Great attention was also given to the land-front, which was completed by October of 1567. In those days, assaults were expected to take place from land. Therefore, Laparelli decided to place the land front on the highest ridge of the peninsula and about a kilometre inland, thus providing full command of the Floriana plateau, which was located some six metres below. The land front was strengthened further by the construction of two enormous cavaliers, four bastions and a series of stone ramparts erected behind the same bastions. A deep ditch was also excavated in the rock below the ramparts, thus separating the new city from the inland and making it near to impossible for the adversary to seize the city. Laparelli's plan included the construction of four additional bastions facing Marsamxett Harbour, and another three overlooking Grand Harbour, connected together by their ramparts. The original intention of Laparelli was to build more cavaliers along the *enceinte* of the city, however only the pair located close to the land-front were completed.

A substantial proportion of the ramparts was built by shaping and sculpting the soft local stone the Globigerina Limestone. Since, the peninsula was abundant with this stone, it became the main building material of this project. In the beginning, the excavated material was reshaped into square blocks and reutilised for the buildings constructed within the city. In fact, the upper part of the ramparts was made up of rows of stone blocks made out of this soft limestone. Other materials such as

A view of the bastions from Hastings Garden

Valletta A PERSONAL CITY GUIDE

wood, lead, steel, implements and provisions had to be imported from abroad.

Thousands of workmen were required to complete this building programme, so foreigners, mainly from Sicily and Calabria, were hired. However, local builders were given preference over foreigners, as they were considered experts in this area. Many Maltese workers, who had previously settled in the southern coastal towns of Sicily, were flocking back, possibly being motivated by the fact that they could earn a regular wage and would be fed well. It is believed that, out of a population of around 30,000, some 4,000 labourers were working on the construction of this city. In addition to the labour force, slaves were also used. Another contemporary historian claimed that during the last months of 1566, no less than 8,000 workmen were working feverishly on the land-front project.

Building the City interior

A basic street plan of Valletta was probably designed some nine months after the Great Siege. After several modifications, it was agreed that a gridiron pattern of streets had to be utilised in the building of Valletta. This layout consisted of one principal, spinal street running from the entrance of the city at the land front, straight down all the way to Fort

THE BUILDING OF VALLETTA

St Elmo, with four parallel streets flanking it on each side, and twelve streets at right angles to it, running from Grand Harbour to Marsamxett Harbour. Laparelli had the unique opportunity of building an innovative city from scratch. The concept of the grid as the ideal town-planning system had been adopted by several 15th and 16th century cities, mainly in the Spanish settlements established in Mexico and South America. Cities such as *Puebla de los Angeles* (now 'Puebla City' in Mexico), were widely copied in the Americas. Clear examples of this typical gridiron design are the cities of Mannheim in Germany, Alckmaar in Holland and Manhattan in New York City.

On the 21 August 1568, exactly eleven years after his appointment day, Grand Master de Valette died, without witnessing the final completion of the city that he had conceived. His successor, the Italian Grand Master, Pietro del Monte, was enthusiastic to keep the construction works moving ahead. He used to visit the building site nearly every day. For this reason, Laparelli designed a new entrance gate that breached the fortification walls overlooking the Grand Harbour, thus making it easier and faster for the aging Grand Master to reach the new city. The new gateway was named *Porta del Monte* (now Victoria Gate), and opened up on to the waterfront facing Fort

Grand Master's Palace

St Angelo, making it possible to access the building site easily after a relatively short boat trip across the harbour. Meanwhile in 1569, after four years in Malta, Francesco Laparelli decided to leave and join the Papal fleet in Messina, Sicily. He would eventually die of the plague on the island of Candia (now Crete). Before leaving the islands for good, Laparelli had spent a lot of time teaching architecture to his main collaborator, a talented Maltese builder called Ġirolmu Cassar.

It is believed that Cassar was born in Malta, either in the Borgo or the village of Gudja, in the quarter of the first 16th century. He had served as a military engineer during the Battle of Djerba (1560) and subsequently offered his services to the Venetian Republic. Then, during the Great Siege of 1565, he had worked relentlessly, repairing the island's fortifications and designing several war machines. After the siege, he built up a great reputation as the chief and resident architect of the Order, also assisting the distinguished Francesco Laparelli. In April 1569, the Grand Master granted Cassar a passport to travel to the Italian peninsula and undergo an intensive study trip. Before leaving, he was given the instruction to study buildings and architectural styles that could be easily imitated on the Island. His study-trip included visits to Rome, Naples, Lucca, and possibly Florence. It is here that Cassar came in contact with the Mannerist style, the main architectural trend of that period.

Mannerism was the predominant architectural style in Italy during the 16th century, from the times of Michelangelo to the beginning of the Baroque era. This style allowed architects to experiment spontaneously with various motifs such as symmetry and harmony, thus challenging the norms instituted during the High Renaissance phase. The Renaissance ideals were subverted as architects started breaking the traditional rules, ultimately creating a type of architecture that was more naïve. Most of Cassar's buildings were designed in the Mannerist style, sometimes also including native features. The heavily rusticated quoins, visible throughout the most significant buildings of Valletta, are clear examples of this style. When Cassar completed his mission in Italy and returned to Malta, the fortifications were almost complete, so he could start focus on the plans of the actual buildings within the City. Buildings attributed to his genius include St John's Co-Cathedral, his unchallenged masterpiece, the seven Auberges or hostels of the Knights, the *Sacra Infermeria*, the Grand Master's (now Presidential) Palace, windmills, several churches, bakeries and private dwellings.

Establishment as the capital city

Five years after the first stone had been laid, on the 18 March 1571, Grand Master del Monte decided to transfer the Order's headquarters from the Borgo to Valletta. The city was far from complete, yet this day epitomised the beginning of a new era for the Knights of St John, and also for the Maltese Islands. After nearly 500 years of history, the Knights had a new permanent abode, and therefore there was no need to search for a better place. Malta, and specifically Valletta, provided the Knights of St John the possibility of surviving and thriving when previously their very existence had been in peril. In return, the Islands would also experience a radical transformation. In 1798, after their 268 years on the Islands, the Knights would leave it in a remarkably different state than the one they had found in 1530. Such a transformation

The *Sacra Infermeria*

Valletta **A PERSONAL CITY GUIDE**

Auberge de Castille (right) and Our Lady of Victory (left)

would not have been possible, had Valletta not been conceived, built and so lavishly decorated and embellished. The capital city of Malta became the new gateway of the Mediterranean, exposing local inhabitants to an influx of different cultures and visitors from all over the world. The 16th century tripartite synergetic enterprise of a French Grand Master, an Italian military engineer and a Maltese architect, had indeed resulted in a great and unique accomplishment. Four hundred and fifty-two years after its birth as a result of a pan-European initiative, the humble city of Valletta is, in 2018, the European Capital of Culture. It shall strive to once again be a protagonist in a bid to create a European influence with ties to contemporary culture.

My Valletta
VINCENT ZAMMIT

Welcome to Valletta – my City! Born, bred, and having lived my youth here, I am still fascinated by Valletta – its culture, history, people and hidden places. Every time I walk the streets of Valletta, I feel proud of the wealth that is all around me. Every street corner is a reminder of times past, of a childhood spent playing in the immediate area of our home, and of the other areas during my teenager years. How is one to start writing down these recollections – is it the name of the street where I used to play? Is it the places that I used to frequent? The historical places around me? The hallowed halls of the palaces and churches that abound? So, take a walk through this city, enjoy it during the day when it is bustling with visitors, or even during the late evenings when Valletta takes on a completely different aspect. Enjoy it and live it, to start appreciating this unique UNESCO World Heritage capital city.

One of the summer activities for many of us was to go swimming beneath the fortifications that surround the city. We used to spend hours there, and there were also self-proclaimed 'family days' – when the whole clan would meet at a pre-arranged place, and we would spend the whole day together. It would usually be past sunset that one would start thinking of crawling back up the hill towards home. Yet, there were evenings better spent with all the cousins and the neighbours' boys and girls running about, playing hide and seek and other street games, and telling stories. Ghost stories were popular, but these were usually told by the adults or the parents, who used them to keep

Valletta **A PERSONAL CITY GUIDE**

us from going too far away from our immediate area. Yet, some of these ghost stories do have a following, while some are also very well known to the public.

One of the first stories that I remember was called 'The Turk Under the Stairs'. It was common in the past to have a statue, usually of plaster, placed in the wide part of the staircase. The main aim was, quite simply, decoration. This statue would usually be of a dark person, dressed up as a Muslim, and the figure would usually be referred to as a Turk. Many people would claim that they heard voices when passing by these statues. There were also 'benevolent' statues, which would leave money for their favourites. Yet, some of these statues were said to have a malevolent streak, with recounted incidents of people falling down stairs after looking at the statues scornfully. Who knows what kind of thoughts used to pass through parents' minds when recounting these stories? Were they meant to keep us from straying far from home, a lesson on the untrustworthiness of strangers?

I clearly remember a family member telling us a story from the times when he was working

Casa Rocca Piccola

as a police officer in Valletta. One evening, while doing the street rounds with another officer, they saw a person who looked very suspicious. The two policemen hurried to question this person, but when they rounded the corner, the person that they were sure they had seen was nowhere to be seen. The interesting fact was that as one rounded this corner, there were no other places, doors, or exits where this person could have escaped. Imagination? Poor lighting and therefore a lot of unexplained shadows? But nonetheless, every time we passed through that place, we looked apprehensively around us, and tended to speed up our pace.

In St Ursula Street, there is the famous story of an English sailor who was invited by a well-dressed female to enter the house. He was impressed by the interior decorations and the treatment he received. On leaving, he remembered that he had left his cigarette case behind him, and on returning on the following day to pick it up, he noticed that the door of the house where he had been was dirty and looked derelict. When he was asked by a neighbour what he wanted, and he recounted the story of having

The bastions and post-WWII dwellings

been inside the evening before, he was told that in fact that building had been closed for quite some time. Yet, when he entered to retrieve his cigarette case, he found it on a table where he had left it – but all the furniture was covered in years-old dust.

There are many stories similar to the above, and every corner of Valletta has a ghost story to tell - some of which tell of friendly spirits, while other spirits are anything but friendly.

My playing ground was *Strada Irjali* (as I knew it in those times, now Republic Street, yet, so many people still refer to this street with the old name) towards the lower end of Valletta. The street's official name was 'Kingsway', but everyone referred to it with the old Italian name. It took me some years before I managed to remember to write the current name rather than the one that I had grown up with. This is the street which runs all along the city of Valletta, and it splits the city into two. Living further downhill from the Palace of the Grand Masters, it was a joy to run around the streets, play all kinds of street games, and enjoy the freedom of the streets. So different from what it is nowadays, when it is almost impossible to find a free parking space. In my time, the few cars that used to pass by, used to be more patient with us running in the streets, as life was actually slower, with no urgency to the appointments that needed to be kept.

Playing in the streets was part of growing up. Yet, during my running around, I became enamoured of the history that surrounded me. As soon as I started to read, I fell in love with history. It took me to places far off, introduced me to adventures and heroes long gone, gave me insight into the stories behind buildings and churches, and gave me the imagination I needed to see myself as one of the protagonists of these events. I often thought, while walking through my precious streets, about the Knights, the soldiers, Maltese heroes and villains and pirates who had passed through the same streets, the same Valletta I call *my* city.

For that reason, I started visiting museums quite early. I remember visiting an important exhibition about the Order of the Knights of St John held in Malta in 1970, an exhibition organised by the 13th Council of Europe. I was just 15 years old, and I could not imagine that there were other materials held by other countries that belonged to the Knights of Malta. I somehow managed to save some money so that I could go and visit this exhibition. I still remember being left in awe at the number of things that I saw. It was now that I started making it a point to visit museums and other exhibitions whenever possible. Usually they allowed me to go in for free – a young teenage boy interested in these things was something quite unusual at that time. And I enjoyed it immensely, as I used to visit these places more than once. The enjoyment of visiting the Palace Armoury (in its original massive hall) practically on my own, as few tourists would be around at that time; the visit to the National Museum, with its archaeological items on the ground floor, and the art collection on the upper floor; Fort St Elmo when it was opened for Maltese people to visit on special days. Finally, at the age of 23, I achieved a dream and started working with the then-Museums Department. Now I had access to all the public places as part of my job, but also to behind-the-scenes collections. My interest

The Palace Armoury

and fascination with history deepened, and guiding people around the treasures that we have in Valletta was always such a wonderful experience.

The National Museum of Archaeology was always one of the most interesting and fascinating places. While information was always readily available, I also used to let my imagination run wild, speculating with my own theories on the artefacts. I was always an avid reader, and so was always up to date with the latest information. The stories that one can tell about the 'sleeping lady', discovered at the Hypogeum, are endless. Why is she resting on a bed? Is she sleeping, dreaming or even dead? Why does part of her hair seem to be shaved? Was she representing a priestess, or a goddess? All these stories grabbed the attention of visitors, along with the various, original, carved stonework from Tarxien Temples, with their intricate designs, spirals, and other decorations. The National Museum of Archaeology has continued to develop even further to this day. There have been more sections added, dedicated to the Bronze Age and to the Phoenician periods. Even here, one can study the different types and styles of human figures as represented by the Bronze Age people, and view the mysteries that surround the few remains, like the menhirs, dolmens and the most enigmatic of all – the cart-ruts.

The Phoenician period is a very interesting part of our history. Although few remains have been unearthed, there are still a few important artefacts. Most important of all is the so-called 'cippus', what we would call a candelabra. Two were discovered in Malta, and one of them was sent to King Louis XVI as a gift. The base of this candelabra has two inscriptions – one in Greek and the other (presumably) in Phoenician. The latter language had been undeciphered for a long time, and it was due to the discovery of these candelabra in Malta that it was possible to decipher this ancient language, making it our very own Rosetta Stone. Nowadays it is possible to translate and understand any Phoenician inscription that is discovered. One of these candelabra is exhibited at the Museum. There are also various other interesting items, such as small amulets and glass objects

MY VALLETTA

and a number of artefacts that were discovered in tombs, besides a replica of a typical rock-cut tomb.

Valletta has other museums, of course. The Presidential Palace, also known as the Grand Master's Palace, houses the famous Palace Armoury and some of the State Rooms are also open to the public. Here one can admire the frescoe-decorated halls telling the story of the Order of St John before they arrived and settled in Malta in 1530, along with the 1565 Great Siege fresco cycle, which depicts the main events of that dramatic summer. It is accompanied by the numerous naval panels glorifying the various victories that were registered by the Order's fleet, and portraits of Grand Masters and other important personalities. The national art collection has been moved to larger premises and here one can observe an interesting collection of paintings ranging from the 13th century to modern times. The national collection contains a good number of canvases by Mattia Preti, the Italian artist who spent 38 years in Malta. Another collection is that of the 18th century French artist, Antoine Favray, whose

Old houses on Independence Square

Valletta A PERSONAL CITY GUIDE

technique in depicting Maltese lace is very typical of him. Through his paintings one can better visualise the interior of houses of the Maltese nobility and their lifestyle. The art collection is varied with a number of good canvases by foreign and local artists alike.

A couple of other museums are concerned directly with war. At Fort St Elmo, which has recently been restored to its former glory, one can visit a refurbished War Museum making use of modern technologies to enhance one's visit. Fort St Elmo is the earliest fortification that was built on the Valletta peninsula, and it faced the onslaught of the Ottoman troops during the terrible summer of 1565. Soon after the defeated Ottoman troops left Malta, its rebuilding was immediately started. Eventually the Fort continued to be added to, throughout the following centuries, with the latest additions being just before the Second World War. Within its halls, a historical depiction of war in Malta throughout the centuries has been set up. It covers the earlier periods down to the outbreak of the Second World War. A private toys museum is located towards the end of Republic Street. Although a small museum, this collection offers the visitors a number of toys that will surely bring back some nostalgia and childhood memories.

Valletta, being the capital city of Malta, also boasts two museums dealing with the banking sector. One of the Maltese banks has set up its own museum, which deals with the earlier history of its predecessors, as well as showcasing various tools, safes, ledgers, portraits and other memorabilia dealing with the Bank's history. The Central Bank of Malta has its own numismatic collection which is on display. The coins that are on display range from the Punic period down to modern times. A Postal Museum has also recently opened. This traces the philatelic history of Malta from the middle of the 19th century till present times. Well set up in an old building, it provides the visitor with the whole collection of stamps, besides a number of artefacts related with the postal service.

Then there are the church museums. The jewel in the crown is the museum attached to St John's Co-Cathedral. Here, one can view, up close and in person, the famous Flemish tapestries, a gift by Grand Master Ramon Perellos to the Church, the silver ornaments, the rich liturgical vestments and important choral books, as well as a number of canvases that used to decorate the church before the 17th century. The Museum also holds two highly prestigious paintings by Michelangelo Merisi, better known as Caravaggio. The other church museum in Valletta is the one in the Collegiate Church of St Paul's Shipwreck. It is located in a large building close to the church, and it boasts various interesting items that were used in times past. There are various items of interest, especially the section dedicated to the various confraternities, which were like social clubs, and even trade unions. One can also find church vestments and other items that form part of the religious rituals carried out in the church.

Each and every church is a museum in its own right. These religious places that abound in Valletta are also particular. There are religious sites belonging mainly to the Roman Catholic Church, but there are also churches of the Protestant faith (which were mainly built in the 19th century), a Greek Catholic Church, and a Greek Orthodox Church. All of these have got their own interesting historical and artistic treasures, which makes Valletta a special place also for religious tourism.

The rich religious heritage that can be seen in Valletta is unique. So many cult places, as well as different historical and artistic heritage, can be seen within the churches. Besides the presence of churches, throughout the year, a good number of religious processions are held. The first procession is held on the 10th February, a national holiday. On this day, the arrival of St Paul in Malta is commemorated. The story, as recounted in the Acts of the Apostles, goes that he was shipwrecked in Malta on

High altar, St Domenic's church

Valletta **A PERSONAL CITY GUIDE**

the way to Rome. The church and the streets are decorated with rich drapery and are a must to visit. During Holy Week, there are various other public manifestations held in Valletta. A number of exhibitions put up by individuals are held, showing small and miniature statues representing the Passion of Christ. On the Friday before Good Friday, a devotional procession is held with the statue of Our Lady of Sorrows. During these days there are a number of interesting works in the churches, with regards to decorations and silver items. In one of the Oratories within the parish church of Our Lady of Safe Haven and St Dominic, a centuries-old tradition is still kept alive. A lavish and artistic Last Supper display is set up within the richly-decorated Oratory belonging to the Confraternity of the Blessed Sacrament. Yet, the main procession is held on Good Friday, when a number of larger-than-life-size statues are carried shoulder high along the main streets of Valletta. These statues represent main events from the Passion of Christ.

The following months host religious processions in honour of St Augustine, Our Lady of Mount Carmel, and St Dominic. In between, there would be other smaller religious processions held by the respective churches to commemorate certain devotions. Throughout these feasts, the churches are a must to be visited, as they are draped in their best attire, bringing out all the damask, the silver artefacts and many other items of rich artistic heritage. In places of honour one finds the statues of the respective saints that are carried out shoulder-high around the streets of Valletta on *festa* night.

I have fond memories of the *festa* of my parish. Being from the parish

Oratory of the Fraternity of Our Lady of Mt Carmel

of St Dominic, I was very much involved as a teenager in helping out with the annual decoration of the streets. The enthusiasm during those days is indescribable. The culmination would be during the week-long feast, when every evening there would be band marches, showered by paper confetti thrown down from the balconies above as they passed through the streets. The solemn procession with the statue of St Dominic being carried around the streets and then the final enthusiastic phase of returning it to its rightful place in the church are deeply-etched in my memory.

It must be pointed out that this is not the only religious heritage that one finds in Valletta. Walking the streets of the city one notices a large number of street niches, depicting different saints. They are also of different shapes and sizes. These type of street niches are to be found all over the Islands, yet the first of these statues were those that were erected in Valletta. The block of housing the Jesuit church, and the old University of Malta building, boasts four large corner statues, all depicting Jesuit saints. These were the first such statues that were erected, and since that time,

St Dominic's church

Last Supper display at St Dominic Priory

hundreds have been set up all over Malta and Gozo. The presence of these niches indicates the various religious devotions of the people living in the area. Another interesting detail to notice is the presence of various names and holy images that can be seen next to the doors of family homes. The names indicate the devotion of that particular family. Instead of putting up just a name, others have added colour by affixing a holy image to the side of their main door. Religious heritage can be seen and felt everywhere.

Valletta is also rich in legends, mysteries and myths. It is not the first time that one is told that beneath Valletta there is a whole new city, with passages following the same lines of the above ground streets. In truth, there are no such underground tunnels that connect all of Valletta, and that another city lies underground. Yet, it is true to say that there are tunnels between certain buildings, and even other underground chambers that are part of the history of Valletta. When Valletta started being built in 1566, it was immediately realised that one of the greatest difficulties in case of a siege would be the lack of water. Thus, it was ordered that everyone needed to have a rock-cut well beneath their homes, in order to preserve the little rain that falls on Malta. The digging of these wells also provided the stones for the building of the houses, while at the same time, providing the necessary water supply to the families. This was not enough, and when later on in the 17th century, an aqueduct had been built and Valletta was thus provided with water, a number of cisterns of varying sizes were excavated in Valletta. These were not however the first cisterns and wells that were dug in Valletta, as before the actual building of the new city, a number of farms had been located in the same area, and they would have had their own wells.

Before the building of Valletta, it seems that the site had a number of natural springs. Nowadays, none of these survived, except for one which is located beneath the Archbishop's Palace. This spring is copious, and it provides water for the Palace itself, as well as for the small garden attached to it. Sometimes, this site is open for viewing, although it is not one which is regularly opened to the public.

The building of the new city also meant that there would be the need for basements, excavated for various reasons. These would also have supplied the building stone. At the same time, they would offer the necessary space for storage purposes. A good number of these underground basements are still in use till this very day. Some are used as workshops, while others are plain cellars.

Still in existence are a number of prison cells dating back from the first law courts that were erected in Valletta. The building was built in the 16th century, and although a new law court was built during the 18th century on the same site, the basement area was retained. It is also obvious that as Valletta was a military defence post, there would also be quite a number of underground passages and chambers within the thickness of the walls. The majority of these are still in existence, but are not open to the public. One such section, which is open to the public, forms part of the 'Saluting Battery and Lascaris War Rooms Complex'. The passage leading down to the war rooms is part of a system that was dug by the British authorities. The underground halls are where the planning for the operations of the defence of Malta, and eventually the invasion of Sicily by the Allied troops, was carried out. These have been restored, and they are open to the public.

Dating back to the war are also quite a few rock-cut shelters which were used by families during the Second World War.

Valletta A PERSONAL CITY GUIDE

They provided temporary shelters during the many air-raids that were launched against Malta from nearby Sicily. Although some of these shelters were small rooms, and meant for one family, there are others which were dug by the authorities, providing shelter to many people still living in the city. Some large houses ended up with their own private shelters as well. One of these lies beneath the rich Casa Rocca Piccola. While part of the shelter was meant for the family members, there was an extension which welcomed the neighbours as well.

Yet the largest underground place where one could take shelter during the war was the railway tunnel, located in the ditch of Valletta. This extended through the whole length of Floriana, and many families found refuge there. By this time, the railway was not in use anymore, and the disused tunnel was turned into a readymade shelter.

Another interesting Second World War shelter, which is not open to the public as yet, is the one that was dug beneath the Governor's Palace, the previous Grand Master's Palace, and presently known as the President's Palace. It is said that this was the place where Winston Churchill, the British Prime Minister and Franklin Roosevelt, President of the United States of America, met during their discussions in Malta before travelling to Yalta.

This information is what one generally finds in various guide books, but it must be said that besides all of these, there are usually more details, corners and other interesting facts to be discovered while walking along the streets of Valletta. Take walks not only within the city, but even outside the city walls, as there is a very good walk beneath the walls that will take one from one side of the peninsula to the other, from Marsamxetto harbour, to Grand Harbour.

This is my city - a city which welcomes one and all. It is where I grew up; where I have run through the streets playing; where I walked the streets to admire and discover its history. It is the city that fostered my love for history. This is my Valletta - where I have participated in its recent history, the political anniversaries and milestones; the happy football days, the summer days, and the local *festa*. This is my city – my Valletta, the *European Capital of Culture 2018*. I welcome you to it – MERĦBA!

Stories of a tourist guide
Bonġu Onorevoli!
VERONICA BARBARA

While guiding in Valletta you meet all sorts of people... fellow guides with their groups, messengers running from one ministry to another, a couple of friends you have not seen in ages, the usual relative who tries to chat you up although you have told him endless times not to stop you when you're guiding. Quite often, my clients notice this and they ask me whether I am so popular, since I keep on waving back at people and responding to greetings. I usually laugh and reply with the cliché phrase that 'In Malta, everyone knows everyone else' since we're such a small country. I also add that Valletta is the main administrative and commercial centre of the Islands. The most important national issues have been decided in Valletta and lives have been made and unmade here in the city. So it is no wonder that, walking along the streets of Valletta, one is always stopping to speak to an acquaintance, making it almost impossible to reach your bus in time for the next trip leaving the city!

Once, however, I had an encounter which startled my clients and, let's face it, was an experience for me too. I was on a usual tour of the Valletta streets with a group of around thirty-five men and women. This Valletta tour allowed them to kill the time until, later in the day, they would join their spouses who were attending a conference at the University of Malta Valletta Campus in St Paul Street. Their backgrounds varied. Some of them were highly interested in architecture and art, whereas others were clearly more attracted to the shopping outlets.

We had just been to the Upper Barakka Gardens and I was

Valletta A PERSONAL CITY GUIDE

leading them back to Republic Street via Castille Place. I stopped in front of the Auberge of Castilla, Leon and Portugal, and had just started to explain about the symbol of the crescent on the coat of arms of Grand Master Pinto, the man behind the financing of the rebuilding of the structure. All of a sudden, a black car drew up in front of us and my group moved to the side. I turned around and saw a man dressed in a dark suit descend the stairs. I knew who he was but my clients didn't.

I quickly informed my group that they were standing on the steps of the Office of the Prime Minister of Malta, the same man who was heading for the car which had just pulled up. He heard me, smiled and, signalling to the driver to wait, he walked toward us to say hello to my clients and shake hands with a couple of them. He didn't stop more than a minute, but all of them were quite excited about it.

When he left, one of them asked me whether it was normal to bump into the Prime Minister and similar high officials in such a manner. I nodded and she seemed surprised. So I started explaining the nature of politics in Malta,

Auberge de Castille

which is substantially influenced by our small size.

For many members of the group, coming from large countries such as the USA and Australia, it is highly improbable that they get to meet members of the country's government in such an informal manner. I found it quite difficult to convince them that politics in Malta and the relationship between politician and voter is a very personal one, with house visits being an extremely essential component of any local political campaign. With two strong main parties and sixty-five Parliamentary Representatives, the political scene in Malta is a hotly-debated topic, even more than football and other sports. When elections are announced, electoral fever is high and life seems to stand still in all other areas until voting day arrives and the decision of the electorate is made public on the following day. Usually the supporters of the winning party spend a whole week celebrating and many outlets remain closed on the Monday following the election, with shop-owners and staff either celebrating in the squares or despairing at home. Although many young people

Republic Street and Palazzo Ferreria

Valletta **A PERSONAL CITY GUIDE**

Café life on Republic Square

are developing a passive stance to politics, this aspect of life still forms an integral part of Maltese culture as is evidenced by the high voting turn-out in elections, always reaching over ninety per cent. Valletta, hosting the offices of the Prime Minister and the President of the Republic, Parliamentary sessions and almost all Government Ministries, serves as the theatre for the political and administrative scene in the Maltese Islands.

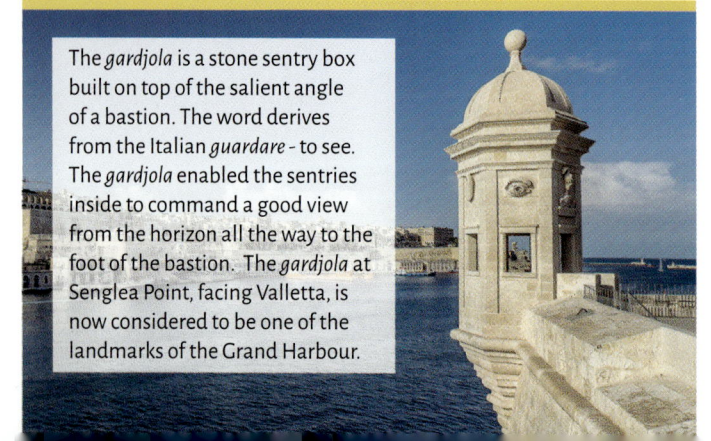

The *gardjola* is a stone sentry box built on top of the salient angle of a bastion. The word derives from the Italian *guardare* - to see. The *gardjola* enabled the sentries inside to command a good view from the horizon all the way to the foot of the bastion. The *gardjola* at Senglea Point, facing Valletta, is now considered to be one of the landmarks of the Grand Harbour.

The Museum of Archaeology
VERONICA BARBARA

Housed within the Auberge de Provence, the National Museum of Archaeology in Republic Street is a perfect showcase of the earliest human settlements in Malta. The display starts on the ground floor and, through authentic artefacts excavated from sites all over the Maltese Islands, explains in detail the life of the very first settlers. These had arrived from Sicily around 7,000 years ago, bringing with them a complex Neolithic culture. As evidenced by bones and other biological remains, they had domesticated animals, namely sheep and goats. Pottery was discovered, along with evidence of fixed settlements. The Museum of Archaeology also displays the earliest animal representation in Malta, showing that this new community had already mastered a degree of artistic expression.

Eventually, the prehistoric community developed a phenomenon, which is very particular to the Maltese Islands, and which earned its people the nickname of 'temple-builders'. The Temple Period, as it is referred to, saw the construction of amazing megalithic structures which are the oldest free-standing structures in the world, older even than Stonehenge and the Egyptian pyramids.

Considered temples by many archaeologists and scholars, given their impressive stature and the effort needed to construct them, such megalithic structures are to be found in different areas of the Maltese Islands, the most famous being perhaps the archaeological park of Ħagar Qim and Mnajdra.

The modern models displayed in the museum help visitors understand the layout and architectural details, as well as

Valletta A PERSONAL CITY GUIDE

Model of the Hypogeum

the chronological development of their plans. Also on display are prehistoric models discovered during archaeological excavations, one of which has, to date, no life-size structure which matches its shape. Such discoveries reveal that the community who built the temples was much more complex than what might be expected. Apart from having a work-force dedicated to construction, as distinct from the work-force focused on rearing animals and taking care of the land, there were also architects, and a kind of selection board who had the right to accept some proposals while refusing others. If we accept the temple theory as being at least very probable, we would also assume the existence of a group of religious leaders (what are often referred to as 'priests' in literature) that took care of the temples and the prehistoric cult in general.

Auberge de Provence which houses of the Museum

THE MUSEUM OF ARCHAEOLOGY

Perhaps the most intriguing of sites dating from the Temple Period is the Ħal Saflieni Hypogeum, situated in Paola. The Museum of Archaeology displays a detailed model of this underground site, allowing the viewer to observe all its levels and intricacies. One of the highlights on display is a beautiful statuette discovered within the Hypogeum. Referred to as the *Sleeping Lady*, it is a true masterpiece of prehistoric art, unique in its kind.

Malta's temple culture was strangely interrupted at around 2,500BC. All evidence of the Neolithic people, whose culture was manifest in impressive megalithic structures and realistic art, disappeared and was replaced by a completely different culture. Referred to as the Bronze Age, this last period in Malta's prehistory is marked by the introduction of metal, and a movement to a more stylistic art representation.

Sleeping Lady

One of the main halls of the Museum

Valletta A PERSONAL CITY GUIDE

Carved stone head

It seems that this new community, not unlike other communities of the era in the Mediterranean region, was very much taken with warfare and fortified settlements. The method of disposing of the dead also changed. Whilst the Neolithic people buried their dead, the Bronze Age people cremated them and built dolmens to house their cremated remains. The upper floor of the National Museum of Archaeology has an extremely didactic display highlighting all the main features of the Bronze Age period in Malta.

A separate area is also devoted to the mysterious phenomenon of the cart ruts, which is still far from unraveled. Many questions remain unanswered when it comes to these channels running parallel along different parts of Malta. How were they created and why were they used? Who created them and during what period? David Trump (2008, 2002), an archaeologist who delved deep into Maltese prehistory and the mystery of the cart-ruts, discusses existing theories and presents an extensive catalogue of these features.

The display on the upper floor of the museum continues from prehistory to history, with the arrival of the Phoenicians and the introduction of writing. Malta's position, strategically placed right in the middle of the Mediterranean Sea, could not be missed by these seafarers known for their extensive trading

Model of a temple

activities. The Phoenicians, and the Punic people after them, brought to Malta many eclectic goods, perhaps the most particular being Egyptian amulets. According to Professor Anthony Bonanno (2012: 15), the ones discovered in the Western Mediterranean, dating from the 1st millennium BC, were Punic reproductions, copying Egyptian techniques and symbolism rather accurately. An example of one such amulet is displayed at the Museum, but blink… and you might miss it! Discovered in an underground tomb in Rabat (Malta), it is one of the tiniest artefacts on display. It is made of bronze, and has a hollow tube topped by the head of the Egyptian god Horus. Inside, a very small sheet of papyrus was discovered. It had a curse, written in Punic script, against the evil spirit that torments the soul of the dead, next to a drawn image of the goddess, Isis. Another very small, and incredibly detailed, amulet that can be admired, is made out of solid gold and consists of images of the gods Horus and Anubis soldered together back to back. Bonanno (2012: 16) gives an extremely comprehensive description of these, as well as of other similar artefacts, placing them in a wider archaeological context.

The Horus Amulet

Malta remained under the sphere of influence of the Carthaginians, until the second Punic war heralded the arrival of the Romans. The display related to this period is extremely informative, with artefacts from both domestic as well as burial contexts. The archaeological record has revealed a very prosperous community, with a thriving urban textile industry, oil production in countryside villas and highly-ornate architecture. Artefacts from these different contexts can be admired at the Museum alongside extensive information.

Given the numerous archaeological sites pertaining to Maltese prehistory and the classical period, it is often the case that visitors to the Maltese Islands do not find the opportunity to visit more than two or three such sites. Although nothing can compare to an onsite visit, a walk through the National Museum of Archaeology offers the short-stay visitor a chance to learn more about the archaeology of the archipelago without visiting all the sites. Being centrally located in the heart of Valletta, it is also the perfect starting point for archaeology enthusiasts who plan to explore as many sites as possible, giving such visitors a wider view of excavated discoveries, connecting one site with another, and thus making a visiting plan much easier to prepare, and more comprehensive. It is also fitting that the archaeology of the very start of society in Malta and its development can be experienced in Valletta, the main administrative, commercial and social centre of the country.

References:
Bonanno, A. (2012) *Apotropaia – Prehistoric and Ancient Amulets from the Maltese Islands, Treasures of Malta*, XVIII:2 (11-18)
Bonanno, A. (2005) *Malta – Phoenician, Punic and Roman*, Midsea Books: Malta
Trump, D. (2002) *Malta – Prehistory and Temples*, Midsea Books: Malta
Trump, D. (2008) *Cart-ruts and their impact on the Maltese landscape*, Midsea Books: Malta

Valletta's international appeal

DAMON ALLEN

I'm so excited to share my passion of Valletta with you. I'm not a native of Malta (born in Canada) but I think you'll find my perspective to be intriguing. I'm not a licenced guide however my business is known as a Destination Management Company, whereby we create full experiences for visitors to Malta. We have offices in Malta, Canada and the US. I can ultimately thank my mother for this writing opportunity since she was born in the village of Paola - about a 10-minute drive from Valletta. My interest in Malta grew as a teenager since I had not yet visited my mother's birthplace. Later in life, and once I became part of the family travel business, I knew that I wanted to include Malta as one of our international offerings for Canadians and Americans. Fast forward to today and my sole work's focus is Malta and consequently, I have relocated here. It perhaps can be seen as a big step but I've had no regrets - which brings me to the point of my interest and what I can convey about Valletta. Since I was not born here I come with a slightly different perspective in how I see things and continue to see them. I'd like to call it the North American perspective. North Americans are hungry for culture and seek out that which is truly unique and authentic. We're not looking for the Italian experience or something that overlaps too much with another culture; we want to be wowed by all things Maltese.

Through my continued endeavours to host North Americans in Malta, I find the best way to appreciate a culture is by hearing stories directly from the people who live here. So you're going to get a bit of first hand experiences with a mix of my perspective on how I see Valletta as having a massive international appeal.

Valletta A PERSONAL CITY GUIDE

Valletta's International Appeal and Present Day Culture

Long before the throngs of inquisitive 20th and 21st century tourists graced our capital city, it had always been an international centre/focal point. Valletta was of course built as a response to the continued threat of the Ottoman Empire – which had been defeated by the Knights of St John in 1565. The design and ultimate construction of Valletta was far more important to Europe than to just Malta. It was regarded as a very strategic archipelago in the defence of the Christian Mediterranean. Thus Pope Pius V and Philip II of Spain worked hard in providing financial support and expert designers such as Francesco Laparelli, the Pope's military engineer, who drew up Valletta's plans and defences.

The Knights of St John, a collection of different tongues from all over Europe, established The City – mindfully crafted to appeal to the many. Its early formative years saw continued investment with the building of magnificent palaces, churches and auberges that housed the Knights.

For the centuries that followed its creation, Valletta continued to be a cosmopolitan style city

The entrance of Valletta with the Tritons Fountain

VALLETTA'S INTERNATIONAL APPEAL

– welcoming people and artists from across Europe. Perhaps the initial kick-start to ensuring a city of people was influenced by Napoleon Bonaparte with his declaration of abolishing slavery; his tenure on the islands was however short and uninspiring to most. Much more openness and prosperity was to come to Valletta, and Malta in general, under the British. Benjamin Disraeli, future British Prime Minister who visited Valletta in 1830, commandingly said that Valletta is "a city of palaces built by gentlemen for gentlemen," and continued with saying "Valletta equals in its noble architecture, if it does not excel, any capital in Europe."

In the 19th century, Valletta became a hive of activity. Consider the Royal Opera House that was built on Republic Street (*Strada Reale* in the day). It invited some of Europe's best opera singers and classical music talents. An open air theatre now sits on the exact footprint of the original opera house – it having been near completely demolished by German aircraft in 1942. It took Malta over 70 years to commemorate a new theatre however it has been a wonderful

A very busy early 20th-century, *Strada Reale*

Valletta A PERSONAL CITY GUIDE

addition to the artistic and recent renaissance of Valletta.

And then we had the famous, or rather, infamous *Strada Stretta* (Strait Street) that welcomed sailors and adventurous travellers alike to Malta's Red Light District at the time. You had people of different nationalities and classes co-existing in the name of a great time – jazz clubs, bars and even brothels. It became known as 'The Gut' among its English visitors. Truly there are many stories to be told about Valletta, past, present and future.

I'm happy to not only share my perspective but also help to tell the story of Valletta through its people.

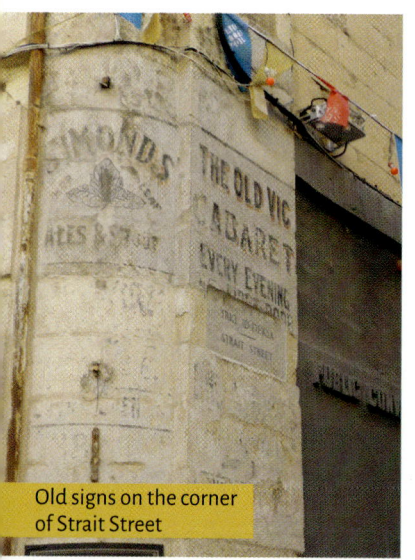

Old signs on the corner of Strait Street

The smell of freshly sandblasted limestone abounds as I enter the main gates of Valletta today. They are putting some of the final touches together to help welcome guests in 2018. And speaking of those main gates (designed by Renzo Piano) - they are saluting all who enter this Baroque capital. Once fully through the gates, one can't but help notice the bustling activity that permeates Valletta on a daily basis. Just the other week, Valletta was welcoming the Croatian Head of State and today there are decorations going up for one of the local church feasts. Malta is a country, which although diminutive in its size, will keep any citizen and visitor busy. The microcosm of that is Valletta - compact and offering a treasure trove of possibilities day and night.

I don't live in Valletta myself, but I come here for inspiration or to get in a mood to work and write. I've been living in Malta for a short period of time however I have been coming and going for years. Travellers can attest that inhabitants of a nation or city often take things for granted. Valletta is an example of the contrary. I am ever so pleased to hear locals who live in and

VALLETTA'S INTERNATIONAL APPEAL

The new parliament building

Valletta **A PERSONAL CITY GUIDE**

outside of Valletta beaming when they speak of *Il-Belt* (The City). I was recently out with a friend and we were trying to decide what to do. There were plenty of options within about a 10-minute drive of our homes. However she recommended Valletta and in her words "There's something about Valletta at night". I smiled. There truly is something about that great capital city of ours.

Monumental legacy, walkability and public spaces
Monuments
Look left, look right, look down the street or across the park. Chances are, you'll find some type of monument dedicated to a time period, a person, a society or even a saint. One of the catchiest things I say to people who want to learn about Malta and Valletta in particular is that Valletta boasts more than 320 monuments in an area of one fifth of a square mile. That makes it one of the most densely populated in the world for monuments. You could truly spend more than three days exploring all of them.

There are the traditional monuments that one would expect representing events. Of these, the most famous ones

Lower Barrakka and the Siege Bell Memorial

(even outside the gates) include: The Victory Bell, Monument to Sir Alexander Ball, War Memorial, Great Siege Monument.

Then at just about every corner it seems you can find a niche memorial that venerate a saint.

And on a grand scale the monuments of Valletta start at its great fortifications that have protected the inhabitants and were once even used to trap the French.

Walkability

Valletta was built upon the Sceberras Peninsula at a time when the only thing that stood upon it was Fort St Elmo. In great part because of the Great Siege Victory, assistance to build this city came from many of the Kings of Europe as well as the Pope's military architect, Francesco Laparelli and later Maltese architect, Gerolamo Cassar. The brand new city was built on a grid format – a departure from the medieval style of winding streets.

I often joke about some of the long and dipping streets as our San Francisco streets. It's really easy to get around with Republic Street being the central divider and the two harbours on either side. You really need to try hard

Where St Lucia Street meets St Ursula Street

Valletta **A PERSONAL CITY GUIDE**

to get lost and if for some reason you do, you easily regroup, find one harbour on one side and then start making your way back to Republic Street. But exploring without a map or guide can be fun because then you'd not be looking for anything in particular. For those that have the time, perhaps an extra day in Valletta, just roam around and admire the different balconies, the niches and all the neat places to eat or have a drink.

Public Spaces
What's really impressive to me is that with the hustle and bustle of Republic Street, one can always duck into a park or garden space to relax. Some might be thinking sure but not at the Upper Barrakka Gardens! Granted, it's not that quiet because it is arguably the best place to get the money shot of the Grand Harbour and the Three Cities but even within it you can duck and relax. Try it! One of my favourite, and almost always quiet spots, is the Lower Barrakka Gardens located near the Hospital of the Knights along *il-Lvant* (East) Street. It's strikingly beautiful – with the imposing monument dedicated to Sir Alexander Ball and the palm trees that surround

Lord Hastings Monument

it. Grab a book or feel free to take a power nap!

A special find (and perhaps it's because it requires a bit more effort) is Hastings Gardens. I've got to be honest, I only discovered it just several years ago when I was coming and going with clients. I have been to a number of events in the evening - and it looks nothing like it does during the day. It's a long park that has many benches to enjoy pure serenity. You'd be pressed to hear just about anything while relaxing here. The views of Floriana, Marsamxett Harbour and the villages across the way are stunning. The only catch is that it is located at the top of the left stairs once you enter the main gates of Valletta. Truth be told, it's not hard to get up there but it's just not on the radar of most travellers. Looking for some chill-out time? Hastings Garden is it.

Present-Day Auberges

When Valletta was established, multi-tongued members of the Order were housed in Auberges or inns. Fast forward to the present day and we are seeing the same thing happen with people from all over the world flocking to Malta and Valletta specifically to

The Garrison Chapel, now the Stock Exchange

Valletta A PERSONAL CITY GUIDE

enjoy the exciting culture. There has been a recent push to build more accommodations in or around Valletta to ensure demand was met. Up until about four years ago, there was not a plethora of options for accommodations. Most people seemed to be staying at one of the fine hotels in St Julians however there were a couple of things that propelled hotel development.

There are a few main factors behind the rise of accommodations. The first and most obvious to me is that Valletta is really cool and a place that people love coming back to, so why not keep them here. The other two factors were the EU Presidency, of which Malta shared honours for part of 2017, and also Valletta being recognised as the European Capital of Culture for 2018.

It's not to say that this boom in development hasn't had its growing pains. There has been much construction going on in and around Valletta to satisfy various needs. I'll often hear the locals complain or being skeptical about all this development. From my perspective, this is a win win for everyone with a bit of pain along the way.

Just the other week, I was walking down St Paul only to discover two brand new boutique hotel properties. I'd like to say I am a person in the know but things are happening so fast that I can't seem to keep up. It truly gets me excited to see how welcoming Valletta is becoming for those who want to be at the centre of culture - bells ringing and the smell of food in the air. It's something to be said that when in Malta, you stayed in Valletta.

Valletta offers a great mix of accommodation styles. Outside

Boutique hotels, Casa Ellul *(above)* and SU29 Sky Villa *(below)*

VALLETTA'S INTERNATIONAL APPEAL

The entrance of Domus Zamittello

the great bastions we find a couple of larger hotels - with only a few minutes walk to the main gates of Valletta. Of special note is the Phoenicia Hotel which just underwent a facelift to open up as a premier luxury hotel. Inside the walls of the City, you can find everything from mid-sized hotels such as Falconeria and the Saint John to Casa Ellul, one of the first glamorous boutique hotels in Valletta, and Palazzo Consiglia which offers hotel style amenities including a spa and pool. Two of my most favourite rooms include the *Piano Nobile* at Casa Ellul and the Grand Harbour Sky Villa as SU29 Boutique Hotel.

And there is a new development slated to open in 2018 that will be perhaps the most exclusive accommodation found in all of Malta called *Iniala* located at St Barbara Bastions in Valletta. We're also seeing a lot of private accommodations in Valletta as well, such as apartments and single bedroom boutique style properties. The options seem almost overwhelming!

Food and other Sociables

I'm a self-professed foodie – with limitations. I eat just about everything except for fish, seafood, organ meats and the beloved *bebbux* (Maltese snails). "Maltese

Valletta A PERSONAL CITY GUIDE

and you don't eat fish and seafood," you're saying to yourself. It's true. Someone clearly dropped me on my head when I was a child. Have no fear, I still know some of the best places to eat fish and seafood from the continued feedback I receive from clients and Maltese alike. The food culture is pretty amazing in Valletta. You can find everything from your ultra-traditional Maltese food to high-end masterfully-designed menus - it's whatever you're in the mood for. Valletta has somewhat modernised over the years but you will still find a few local bakeries working around the clock as well as grocery stores with fruit and vegetable stands - an expectation in a Mediterranean country.

I often hear former travellers to Malta presenting the food as not being all that palatable. My follow up would always be, "When exactly did you visit Malta?" We are a food mecca with new restaurant after new restaurant trying to outdo the previous new find. There is a budget for any taste. Some of the more popular restaurants sometimes have to be booked a week or more in advance for lunch, they're that good. But what's more than the food is the personalities that go

Upper Barrakka Gardens

along with them. Take Da Pippo on Melita Street for example where there are no formal menus. The servers almost tell you what to eat – they're so convincing and charming.

I couldn't even put my finger on the exact number of restaurants one can find in Valletta but whenever you're hungry, you're covered. In addition the Maltese delights, one can find everything from steakhouses to pizzerias as well as 'timed seating' restaurants. I had a craving for Chinese dumplings the other month and sure enough I was covered at Sesame Dim Sum and Noodle Bar. For casual eats I love Jubilee on St Lucia Street and Nenu the Artisan Baker Restaurant. Located on St Dominic Street, Nenu is housed in an old bakery. It offers traditional Maltese fare through its extensive menu. Of special note is the *ftira* which is kind of like a flatbread pizza but it's not pizza. You can see everything from the hot baked *ftira* to the simple sandwich *ftira* filled with beans, tuna, tomatoes and more! There's even the cheap, tasty and iconic *pastizzi* snack that can be enjoyed at Champs on Melita Street (among other establishments).

The Preca sisters have two restaurants that can satisfy every need and include Kings Own Band Club Restaurant on Republic Street and Palazzo Preca on Strait Street. Some of the newer and cool restaurants include Taproom (set timed seating for dinner) on Old Theatre Street as well as Panorama (oh that view) on St Ursula Street.

Valletta has everything for anyone on any food budget. The upscale restaurants truly shine through with Michael's, *Il-Ħorża*, Palazzo Preca, and Harbour Club to name a few. Harbour Club on Quarry Wharf is my personal favourite right now (it changes). The simple but elegant feel is welcoming and if you're in Valletta at the right time of year, you'll be dining outside with a view of Fort St Angelo across the harbour or of Victoria Gate in Valletta. The service and food are exquisite.

Searching for sweets or a fine cup of coffee? My favourite places include the chic Charles Grech or Caffe Cordina, both on Republic

Valletta A PERSONAL CITY GUIDE

Street, and old school Prego, on South Street. Charles Grech is my go to for Americanos in the city whereas Caffe Cordina is just all around amazing. Cordina is the oldest coffee shop/bakery in Valletta offering full menus, and gorgeous outdoor seating in Piazza Regina. No one who comes to Valletta misses Caffe Cordina. And I've got to thank our Italian friends for some of the fresh pasta bars and... oh that gelato! The most divine *gelato* can be found at Amorino – started by two Italian friends in Paris. We are very happy to have them in Valletta (my selfishness coming across?).

Got a craving for a beer or cocktail? Nothing is too far to enjoy in Valletta. For beer, my top recommendations are the Beer Cave, 67 Kapitali, Café Society and Jubilee Café. For Scotch the crown goes to StrEat Whiskey Bar and Gin at Yard 32 – both located on Strait Street. Great local and foreign wine can be enjoyed at the many restaurants as well as at Ellul Wines and Spirits, Charles Grech and Trabuxu Wine Bar (order a platter or two). For an ingenious cocktail, head over to Lab Crossover Bar on Strait Street.

Needless to say, there are endless possibilities for food and drink in Valletta!

Faith In 'The City' –
a perspective with Dr Ivan Grixti

A few years back I happened to be in Valletta on Good Friday of the Easter Week. I had seen a Good Friday procession in the village of Paola before so I was looking to see one in the capital city. This procession took place from Our Lady of Jesus (*Ta' Ġieżu*) church in St.John Street which is located on the east side of Valletta close to the Grand Harbour. When I arrived, the procession had already started but I was still able to get a good spot on the very narrow St Ursula Street. A couple of things struck me as being different or unique from the one I had witnessed previously. One thing for sure was the somberness of it; surely one would expect this in a Good Friday procession but it felt different. Another thing that struck me and it's something that has been with me for over three years now - is one or more gentleman with a noticeable hump or callus on their back. I had later asked someone in Valletta about the noticeable hump on the gentlemen to which the person responded "It's from carrying the statue." I was truly

VALLETTA'S INTERNATIONAL APPEAL

amazed and this is something that has stayed with me up until now – until I had a chance to write about what I saw and to investigate further into faith representation in Valletta.

Valletta boasts over 25 churches or places of worship– for a population of approximately 5,700 people. Not only will you find churches of the Catholic faith but also those of other Christian denominations, namely St Andrew's (Scots) Church and St Paul's Anglican Pro-Cathedral. St Andrew's is a cooperation between the Methodist Church and the Church of Scotland and they practise based on the Reformed Christian tradition. St Paul's has Pro-Cathedral status because although it is not a 'main' Cathedral, it shares cathedral status and is one of three cathedrals of the Anglican Diocese of Gibraltar in Europe. The Catholic churches in Valletta are spectacularly embellished - it's truly hard to describe any of them in simple terms. Take St John's Co-Cathedral, the church of the Knights of St John, where art almost supersedes faith. I'll often hear "... not another church to visit" from visitors. Well of course, it's much more than a

St Barbara's church

church and deserves an ample amount of time to understand all of its representations – from the side chapels, to the tombstone laid flooring, to the altar, painted vaulted ceiling and to the famous Caravaggio pieces that adorn the oratory. Simply put, St John's is a site, and a sight, to be seen.

With St John's taking the crown and it being the only church in Valletta that charges a fee to visit for touring purposes, it surely isn't the only one worth visiting. Consider St Paul's Shipwreck Church and its relics, the Carmelite Church with its domed ceiling, to Our Lady of Victories Church, the first church and first building to be completed in Valletta.

I could go on, but I'm interested in presenting something compelling about faith in Valletta – which brings me back to my first paragraph.

Three years had passed and I was in search of one of the gentlemen with the noticeable hump on their back. There had to be a neat story there. I recalled that the Easter Good Friday procession was organised by Our Lady of Jesus (*Ta' Ġieżu*) church, run by the Franciscan minors. However I had been out of luck on a few occasions seemingly thinking I could just drop in for a visit. On my third casual attempt, I arrived nearing elevin in the morning to find that the church was open and preparing for Mass. I encountered a gentleman and explained my intention to find one of the gentlemen that I had witnessed. Thankfully he knew what I was asking for however he had to make a few phone calls to find out who would be the best person to talk to. "I'll find you the big one" he said. I can't lie, that excited me. "Noel Grixti, the big one". So we had a name but we needed to locate the number. He flipped page by page through his handwritten telephone book about four times without any success. "One more time". Thankfully that one more time located the mobile number of Dr Ivan Grixti.

As I do with most people I am interested in meeting, I googled Dr Grixti. I found out that he is a lecturer at the University of Malta, specialising in Accounting as well as once having ran for the European Parliament. I couldn't really find out anything to do with his interest in faith other than a post on his Facebook page referencing "Breeding tomorrow's statue bearers … ." Ok I had my

VALLETTA'S INTERNATIONAL APPEAL

Church of the Jesuits

guy. All I needed to do now was to meet with him to hear his story.

I arranged to meet Dr Grixti at Casa Ellul Boutique Hotel for a meeting. I gave him a little background about myself to break the ice and of course my interest in speaking with him. "I was raised here and I am currently living here", he says. His mother was born in Valletta in 1936 in lower Republic Street. His dad is from Sliema and when his parents married in 1959 they had already gone to live in Sliema. Ivan's grandparents on his mother's side were still living in Valletta and both were ill. He recalls how his mother and sisters took care of them until they both passed away. Part of the roster meant staying two nights a week in Valletta with his mother.

Growing up in Valletta he recalls him and his brother and himself getting involved into "the very interesting hobby of church decorating" at St Dominic's church. His mother's cousin's family was charged with decorating the interior of the church for all liturgical feasts – Christmas, Easter, the main feast among others. While his mother and father were helping take care of his grandparents, his brother and himself found an escape in this church decorating. "Instead of playing waterpolo, we got into church decorating". Ivan says that even his son is now into church decorating.

Dr Grixti worries about the future of supporting the faith in Valletta. With all that is going on in Valletta with the celebration of Capital of Culture status, refurbishments and the like, he says "Valletta is a dying city". I've got to be honest, I was kind of shocked to hear that. He put it into perspective for me. The population of Valletta has gone from approximately 25,000 people to just under 6000. With over 26 places of worship and all the upkeep and support that is needed, I quickly understood what he meant; he was worried about the churches in Valletta. From my perspective, this is a world phenomenon with many of the big cities losing their inhabitants to the suburban areas in a big way. He suggests that the government make it more attractive for families to move to Valletta by providing some subsidies thereby encouraging people to move back. That surely would help propel the church support he surmised. He recognises the importance of the new restaurants, bars, hotels and festivals but moving back to Valletta can be out of reach save for expats with more disposable income.

Besides from the depopulation of Valletta, he points to the parochial rivalry that exists - not only in Valletta but throughout the islands. Supporters of one church do not often take part in festivities of another. In the same way, band clubs and their members do not often take part where another band club supports a parish church. Of course we both recognised that this shouldn't be the way it is since all were ultimately supporters of the catholic faith. He personally suffered a lot because he tried to build bridges over the years. "This is the Good Friday Procession of Valletta so we should all support it," he says. "We can all get behind the Valletta Football Club but then there are these issues". For him personally - he managed to be a bridge in being President of a band club that is not a supporter of the Good Friday Procession while he participated in carrying statues in the procession.

We start to dive into his personal passion with statue carrying. It's roughly 1.2 miles.

St Paul's Shipwreck church

Valletta A PERSONAL CITY GUIDE

"I do it with devotion. In fact so much so every year I have a different intention". He recalls that one year a friend of his had a break up and because his fiancèe was so taken aback, she attempted to harm herself by overdosing on medication. He suggested to his friend that he could be at the hospital and just wait or join in prayer at the Good Friday Procession. The vow that Ivan made that year was to heal the pain and suffering of his friend's fiancèe. "It was life or death" he says. He simply wrote her name on a piece of paper and placed that paper at the base of the cross that was part of the statue he was to carry. He recalls looking at the knees of the statue of Jesus and feeling compelled at that moment to run inside the church and write down her name and place it at the base of the cross. "We performed a miracle that day. She survived. She came back to her senses".

He has been carrying statues for 29 years – next year will be his 30th. "To be honest with you, I've already planned to step aside" he says. To him, this is like professional football. "There are an amount of years when you're good at but something then you have to be a gentleman and that's it." There

Our Lady of Sorrows procession

are eight statues and each one has its own intricacies and own weight. He began to carry statues even before he considered it serious – so adding to his 30 years. He carried one particular statue 'Behold the Man' for 11 years straight. He says it is carried by six men and weighs 400 kilograms. Ivan says that for those who do well with this particular statue, there is a great likelihood that that person will do well with the crucifixion statue. His 'buddy' and he carried the 'Behold the Man' statue together for years and now they share the honour of carrying the crucifixion statue. "I'm left wing, my buddy is right wing".

The parochial rivalry has forced them to seek out statue bearers from outside of Valletta. Nonetheless, he believes the Good Friday Procession to be a very big deal. "I have this vision that the Good Friday procession in Valletta could be like what the Passion Play is to Oberammergau, Germany". It's serious he exclaims. In Valletta they don't have food vendors or people selling souvenirs. They are even serious about how the statue-bearers enjoy a sip of water. Instead of taking a number of steps and then putting the statue down, the bearers walk from street corner to street corner. Ivan and his team even consult the oldest texts to ensure they are doing everything properly and not injecting characters into the procession that do not have any direct relevance. They even have committees that vote on any alterations or changes. Once they had rejected the donation of a new statue to add to the eight. It goes back 350 years in referencing that the eight selected must remain eight.

It's time for me to zone in on the callus that has formed on his back from carrying the statues. The crucifixion statue weighs nearly over a ton carried by ten men. He confesses that it's not an easy feat. He stresses that carrying the statues in Valletta during this procession, they move from street corner to street corner with the band moving in one way and the bearers moving in another way. "Sometimes I close my eyes thinking about having to walk so far and even uphill still." He's actually very thankful to have the callus. "Once you get used to the weight, this becomes so hot with the friction of the wood, you can practically take any weight". He confirms that other gentlemen carrying the statue have calluses as well. He says it is a phenomenon. "Most statue bearers in Valletta have some form of this."

After Valletta 2018, Dr Grixti says that although he will not be participating as a bearer, he will be involved. "I'm going to do surgery to remove this", he says. I ask him if he wears it as a badge of honour. He answers me this way: "I'll answer your question this way. I would prefer dying with it". He has a smaller callus that he will retain so the significant physical reminder of his immovable devotion will not be completely removed.

The People of Valletta
Jean Paul Mifsud - Investigative Journalist and Entrepreneur

I was put in touch with Jean Paul by a friend who thought talking to him would make for an interesting sit down. Jean Paul splits his time between Malta and Ragusa, Sicily. He and his wife run a company called Barbuto Natural Foods whereby he exports foods such as olive oil and other products produced from his farms in Sicily to Malta. But he also wears another hat or two; he is known in Malta circles as an investigative journalist who has covered events such as war zones, disaster stricken areas and also programmes on human trafficking to uncovering scandals. He's got this distinct look which is also found as the main image of Barbuto. It's like part farmer – part bohemian. There's probably something else in there but I can't pinpoint it at the moment. He wears a distinctive hat and has a good amount of beard to round the look out. I met Jean Paul at his Palazzo on St Ursula Street in Valletta. He has converted it into a youth hostel. His palazzo withstood the war - it was one of the few that was not hit by a bomb. It was built in the 1570s and owned by one of the Cotoner brothers who were both Grand Masters of the Knights of St John.

"I'm a Valletta boy", he says. He grew up in an apartment opposite the main door of St John's Co-Cathedral. As a boy in Valletta, he would read books but he would also love to run around exploring everywhere. People say Maltese people have day jobs and also hobbies. Well Jean Paul has more than one hobby. The main thing that piqued my interest was his work on the underground tunnels of Valletta. "With Valletta, I would say we are maybe four or five people who actually experienced underground Valletta on their

VALLETTA'S INTERNATIONAL APPEAL

skin," he says. That's when I began to lean in because I was so intrigued to hear what he what he was going to say next. He says it was fun in the beginning. He remembers running into these tunnels as a kid and not knowing where he would exit. He would tell his mother that he was going to study - and according to him it was. He says that it is a 'myth' that there is a city beneath a city and the true function of these tunnels was for drainage. Back in 2007, along with other highly skilled team members, he created a 3D map of Valletta - from the era of the Knights until the present time. His idea was to create a time machine whereby someone could walk around Valletta with special glasses and see images of old Valletta. And this was before Google Glasses!

He shows me his map that outlines waterlines and sewers. He said the Knights took defence to a different level. Instead of building Valletta like Mdina with its winding roads, they decided on the grid pattern with sharp corners. "Prepare a good fortress on the outside. Build two levels of bastions so you can defend against sea and land attacks. The Knights ensured that Valletta was well supplied with water so there

One of the few remaining green grocers in Valletta

are a plethora of wells or cisterns with their own storage. It was like having gold". He continues by showing me diagrams of wells and the whole physiology of the process whereby water would arrive from Rabat along the Wignacourt aqueduct. He points out on the map where he likes to access these tunnels. He says a good idea s decade ago was to make these underground access points public but there were practical issues such as wires, wheelchair access and others. He said there was talk about a legend that connected the Grand Master's Palace to Marsamxett Harbour. There was this older gentleman who told Jean Paul of an access point he remembered when he was younger. Unfortunately Jean Paul and his team were unable to locate it since the lower part of the Palace was concreted over when a central bank was located there. He says, "The legend holds a bit of water because Grand Master Vilhena likely would not have walked through the streets to get to the Manoel Theatre. He could have used a direct passageway." There is a further legend perhaps that says that there might have been a direct link to Manoel Island, he intimates.

Sister Agnes Zammit - Mother Superior at the St Ursula Convent
In not wanting to tell Valletta stories from similar perspectives, I ventured over to St Ursula Street to see if I could capture a very interesting interview. St Ursula Street is the site of the Monastery of St Ursula. I had heard that cloistered nuns lived there and thought that interviewing a cloistered sister would be most interesting. I had passed by a couple of times only to find the door closed. After enjoying my favourite coffee at Charles Grech on Republic Street, I proceeded to walk towards the Monastery. On my way to it I ran into the father in law of my cousin who owns a clothing store in Valletta and runs the Malta Music Awards. I told him that I was going to try to interview a sister at the Monastery and he said "I don't think you're going to get in there. They're cloistered". Well I was hoping today would be my lucky day as I recalled that the Monastery actually had opening hours.

At about ten to eleven am, I entered the open door and walked upstairs. I found a fairly plain room with these interesting cage-like windows with thick wooden or interconnecting iron ribbons that spanned the entire window. Over to my right were two ladies and a man and they were speaking to a nun through one of these meshed windows. The man was enjoying a local Cisk beer (which I thought was hilarious) and they were all engaging in dialogue. The people asked if there was something I needed. I said I wanted to see if I could talk to a nun about this place and ask a few questions. It turned out that the people were family of the nun and that they were from Gozo and Australia. My request was answered by the sister saying, "Let me get Mother Superior". She told me to wait on the other side and sit on the bench which was facing the other window. Within minutes Mother Superior arrived with a warmth that took away any nervousness that I might have had. Her name was Sister Agnes Zammit. Here was my chance to find out as much as possible about her and the nuns that live here.

Not knowing exactly my line of questions I asked "Where are we right now? What is this place"? Sister Zammit had entered the monastery as a nun when she was 18 years old; she is 58 years now. I told her that I was writing about Valletta from different

Coat of arms on St Ursula's church

perspectives - through the people that lived, worked or were born here. Her response to living in Valletta was interesting to me. She said "Life is very good in Valletta". It was perhaps a little off to me because she is cloistered and does not go outside. So I'm thinking, "How exactly would you know?" but I paused and just listened. She was talking from the perspective of the people of Valletta; they give them charity, help them in the church. Namely she was speaking about a group of supporters of St Paul's Shipwreck Church and *Ta' Ġieżu* Church, both located nearby.

"We come from Jerusalem", Sister Agnes explained. That got me really going and then I started to put two and two together. Their website is run by the Order of St John (Knights of Malta). The monastery was established shortly after the Knights of St John arrived in Malta - first in Birgu where the Knights had their home base. Their close connection with the Knights is displayed when they celebrate the feast of the Blessed Gerard (founder of the Order) in the church of St Ursula on site. I personally remember visiting this church during Easter on Maundy Thursday when the religious function of the Seven Churches takes place. In visiting the church, one can see relics of Blessed Gerard – namely his skull. Taking it a bit back with a history lesson, the Blessed Gerard was from the Benedictine order that was appointed rector of the hospice or hospital in Jerusalem in 1080 and consequently became the founder of the Order of St John.

There are 12 sisters that live here with the youngest being 27 years old and the eldest 87. They do not leave the monastery unless a family member is in the hospital or on the occasion of an election to vote. When sister Agnes was young, she wanted to give her whole life to Jesus. She saw other nuns running in the streets and in the shops. That wasn't for her; it was a life of full devotion to Jesus that she was after. She says they are very happy here. They have an amazing roof with large tables where they enjoy dinner, play cards and also bingo. I betcha they have an amazing view too! Although they don't see the development and ongoings within Valletta, they hear and read about it in the news. When people visit they share news and gossip. For Sister Agnes, she reads the church news and all of the nuns are without internet. They have a good number of computers within the Monastery but she relays that even with the youngest nun, they all want to be free of the internet. The group however has a Facebook page and a Father William runs it by posting something from time to time.

I brought up the Benedictine cloistered nuns in Mdina - looking for some differences. She said that Jesus called them to be in Valletta and that is the main difference. Bringing up the Benedictine order was a good bet because it led to her sharing a memory last year where the nuns travelled to Mdina to share in a procession. "We went to Mdina at nine in the morning and joined the other sisters. We made confession to a priest that we didn't know and then we took a pilgrimage through the streets of Mdina". They were in full uniform she says – meaning that they had the emblem of the Knights on their cloaks. Tourists were taking pictures of them saying "Oh the Knights of Malta", she laughs. What followed was a Mass, a touring of the Carmelite Church museum and a dinner at her 'real' sister's house. Other cases in which the sisters have been outside of the convent for special reasons include the visit of the Pope and also trips to Jerusalem and Lourdes with the Knights of St John.

Sister Zammit was born in the village of Żebbuġ 'in the square' and has two sisters with large families. Her favourite food is spaghetti with rabbit stew. Each of the sisters cooks and takes turns. Their typical day includes waking up at five in the morning and mostly praying with meditation. They do have free time throughout the day at certain hours when they play the piano or guitar or do restoration works. Complete silence time is between one and two in the afternoon. The importance of prayer to the sisters within the monastery is highly connected with the country. When the Knights were fighting, they prayed for them and the country to be victorious. Now they pray for the strength of the religion in the country.

I hear a bell ring in a distance so I begin to wrap up the impromptu interview. She tells me (again) that her English is not good and that I should take out the mistakes. I reassured her that I thought her English was perfect and we had a laugh. "Please close the door behind you".

Valletta A PERSONAL CITY GUIDE

Dr Peter Carbonaro - Notary

In Canada where I was born, when we think of a notary – the certification of documents comes to mind. When I was applying for my Maltese ID card I had to go through a number of steps which included certification and one of my choices was to visit a notary in Valletta. Peter Carbonaro is a third-generation notary located in the narrow Old Treasury Street. Outside of his office, you can see the names of his father and his grandfather; it is the exact office that has been used for three generations. Each time I visit him he is quite busy. When I was finally able to steal some of his time away, I proceeded to ask him about his roots in Valletta – but he stopped me midway in saying "I don't know how deep-rooted you think I am. I wasn't even born in Valletta. I was born in Sliema." But clearly he is deep-rooted. His father's family and father's father's family have all been from Valletta.

His grandfather died in 1929 when there were very little social services around. "It was a time of great hardship just before the crash," he proclaims. He left a widow and three very young children. In 1954, his father graduated from University and

Notary Carbonaro's office in Old Mint Street

succeeded in the legal business up until he died suddenly in 1990 which is when Peter took over the office.

A notary in Malta is different from the type of notary found in the US and Canada. Here a notary is a general lawyer who can do anything such as the involvement in selling a property, liquidation of estates - essentially everything that does not require an appearance in the courts for litigation purposes. Dr Carbonaro didn't want to enter the legal field. He wanted to do everything except the law. At the time when he was at university, there were not a whole lot of options for him so he was 'generally' pushed in this direction. He got set in his ways so he stayed put.

On the wall, there are transfers dating back to 1910. He has even had requests that he needed to pull from a bound book from 1923. To my eyes, it's lovely nostalgia but it is also a complete working office with all the visible elements. The original transfer records were all kept at Government Archives in Valletta but unfortunately the archives received a direct hit by an enemy bomb and most of the records were destroyed. So the records he has pre-WWII are the only ones that exist. Marriage contracts, sale of a boat – everything was done by notaries in those days. "The notaries of Malta are the most trusted branch of the legal profession".

Pictures on the wall are from Valletta in 1890. There is one picture of the parish church of Żejtun on his wall. He says he does a lot of work there and when people from Żejtun come to his office in Valletta, they find the picture comforting. He also has a picture of a graduating class from 1910. In the photo is his grandfather as well as his wife's grandfather.

I had pointed out that I thought his last name was not a common Maltese surname however he said it was more so these days. He had a visitor from Salerno who mentioned that his last name was common there. He got the impression that the people with the surname were rather "notorious" or "fisherman as they say".

During his youth, he fondly remembers the Independence Riots, Easter devotions and running around to various offices with his day. He loves working in Valletta. It's "the buzz" as he puts it. He has his favourite places for coffee such as Caffe Cordina

Valletta **A PERSONAL CITY GUIDE**

where they get his drink ready as soon as they see him. For lunch, it's whatever strikes his fancy. He sees himself doing this until he dies. He has no hobbies.

I asked him what his thoughts were of Valletta 2018. "They are bold" he says. He is thankful because of the infrastructure money that has become available to move things along faster. He ends our chat by saying that there are perhaps more colourful people in Valletta than cultured ones.

Renato Zampa - Jeweller:
"Live from Times Square," is how I opened the discussion with lots of chuckles that followed. I have known Renato for some time. I first became aware of him and his family through my mother's cousin's husband who worked with him. I have this saying in Malta - If I am looking for someone in particular but don't know how to get a hold of the person, I always say "I have a cousin...". It's so true. Malta is so small that connections are an ask away.

Renato was born in Valletta on Merchant's Street in front of St Dominic's Church. He doesn't live in Valletta anymore but I joke with his wife who, is present, that "he wants to move back".

Typical Maltese silver filigree

VALLETTA'S INTERNATIONAL APPEAL

"It's true," he follows up. His family has been in the jewellery business for over 200 years. He is the sixth generation, with his son, the seventh, also being in the business. The first Zampa arrived from Rome as a jeweller. The Government of Malta at the time was looking for an authority or a consul in jewellery to stamp gold as an official appraiser. "All gold had to be stamped".

I mention that there are a multitude of Zampa jewellery stores in Valletta. "They are all my relatives," he exclaims. His family started opening shops in Valletta back in about 1830. Renato said he had no choice, it was the family business. His father, now in the business for 73 years, started when he was just 14 years old because his father had died. Most of the family shops are located on St Lucia Street. During World War II, the area was flattened and they had to rebuild their stores.

Some of his fondest memories of growing up here include swimming at the Valletta Waterpolo Club. People sometimes used to say that he was born in the pool. His father used to play on the Valletta team. The club is still there and is located on the Marsamxett side of Valletta. When he was 18 years old, he met his wife "just down the road" on St Paul's Street next to the church.

It was a big deal to say you were from the city. They were and still are very proud.

I mention the new renaissance we are seeing in Valletta and the capital culture designation. He recalls the sailors walking past his family's shop on St Lucia Street on their way to Strait Street. That occurred up until 1979 which was when the British Navy left our islands. He recalls the central meeting place of Republic Street, walking up and down to find a date.

He spends 11 hours in Valletta, arriving at 8am and departing at 7pm. When he wants to go out to eat, he will often come back to Valletta for dinner. "We are so proud of it, I love it", he says. He moved from Valletta at the age of 25 to Gżira where he still resides to this day. I point out that Gżira is maybe about an 11 minute drive to Valletta so why all the fuss? He loves all of the activity in Valletta. Renato points out that back in the 90's there were about 20,000 people living in Valletta. Nowadays there are 6,000 or so people living here. "They left in those days because everyone wanted to go

Valletta A PERSONAL CITY GUIDE

out from Valletta. "Now everyone wants to come into Valletta."

He loves all of the development that is going on especially with the boutique hotels being built. It's bringing even more people into the city which is good for the city and for his business.

I ask Renato about his hobbies. He said before it used to be water polo, football, politics and the like. But now it's "eating and drinking wine". Sounds like a good hobby to me.

Alfred Azzopardi - Tailor:

When I moved to Malta, I needed to get my ducks in order. I needed to find my favourite grocery store, my dry cleaner, car wash - my go tos so to speak. Last year I needed some alterations done since I had lost a bit of weight so I did a Google search and made some phone calls. I had been living in Senglea at the time so I was searching for something that was relatively close. A few of the numbers I called kept on ringing whereas another gentleman in a neighbouring city was too busy with work from a film set. I was able to locate a few tailors in Valletta so I set out with a bag of clothing in hand. There was a name that popped up a few times,

A draper's shop in Valletta

Alfred Azzopardi, so I honed in on him.

Alfred's shop is located on St Lucia Street, further down towards the Marsamxett Harbour side. You'd know you found the spot because there is a 'Tailor' sign jutting out from the building. As I approached the shop, I could see a gentleman in the doorway, smoking a cigarette. "Alright?" he said to me in a raspy voice. I responded with the equally pleasantly-toned "Alright". For those who don't know, saying "Alright?" is the quickest way of asking how you're doing in Malta. Just listen for it; it's everywhere. I knew that this guy was good because he had a lot of work and I could see that he had pants on his workbench that he was creating for customers. It's a small shop but very adequate. I had recalled hearing from my cousin's husband that his grandfather's sister's husband Alfred (following me?) is a tailor and located on St Lucia Street. I proceeded to ask Alfred if he was the one and he said "No, that's the other one". There is actually another tailor named Alfred just 50 steps up from Alfred Azzopardi - about 10 years his senior.

My first priority was to ask Alfred some questions because he didn't have any customers (besides me) at the moment. He starts at seven in the morning but says he doesn't have to start that early – it's a habit. He was born in Valletta in 1947 on 22 July and resides in the village of Msida where he moved there when he was 27. He takes the bus every day. He's actually never driven a car because he's never felt the need to have one and because he was always too busy to take a break to learn. He said he used to drive a motorcycle but that was years ago. Tailoring for him now is a bit of a hobby - it passes the time and puts a bit of money in his pocket. He met his wife on Republic Street (known as Strada Reale or Kingsway in those days). He says, now people go to meet in Paceville (the major club district in Malta) but before it was Kingsway.

Alfred's father was also a tailor and they worked together in the same shop for about 40 years. Alfred recalls the time when Valletta was more populated. The sailors and Maltese alike would walk from Caffe Cordina area and where the Wembley shop is located. He would go out with five or so friends and they would hang out at Café Premier which was located in Piazza Regina. For him, it's special to be from Valletta. When he was young, he stuck to Valletta. Venturing into Floriana, just outside the main gates of Valletta, might see him and his friends in a fight because of the local football rivalry.

He has all kinds of customers. He used to make suits (and still knows how to make them) but he prefers to only make pants on special request. He recalls the time when he would work with the highest quality fabrics but not much remains for purchase on the island.

He recalls the time when he used to do alterations for the Navy but through another store located on Old Bakery Street. He would charge £25 and then the other store would mark up the charge for the customer to £50. Of special note was an alteration made for Lord Mountbatten, he recalls. He made it a point to say that he is fair to everyone. Whether it is for Maltese or British persons, he charged the same. He doesn't have any plans to retire – he just figured when he doesn't want to do it anymore he'll stop. In the summer he works until 2pm whereas in the winter months he stays on until 4pm.

I ask Alfred if he ever goes on vacation. He says, "I go to Gozo". He has never left the country. He says he doesn't know why exactly he hasn't left the country. He said he has everything he needs in Malta. But he tends to stay away from crowds unless it is to the village feast in Msida.

Doris Cusens

In searching for interesting people to engage within Valletta, it dawned on me that a lot of the people in my list were men. Of course, there were plenty of women to engage however I was looking for a more prominent figure or rather one that impacted Valletta in a way that perhaps shaped it and consequently Malta as a whole. Believe it or not, it was on Mother's Day in 2017 that I found the exact person I had been looking for. A couple of months prior, I had listened to a lecture by a Mr. Simon Cusens on The Women of Malta in World War II.' I thoroughly enjoyed hearing of the great impact that Maltese women had and essentially in helping run the country – something that normally have been cast off as an improbability in those days. I had contacted Simon to see if he would have a recommendation for me. Within half a minute of messaging, he knew who I should be meeting. In his words, "You may wish to speak to a 71 year old Valletta lady, former TV and radio personality and philanthropist for many years, tour guide for VIPs in her later years and pioneer of fitness for women between 1971 and the 1990s, having been awarded the MQR medal by her country for women's emancipation in 2008…". Of course my interest had not only been piqued but I think I had found exactly what I had been looking for, Simon went on, "She won the 'Tourist Guide of the Year' award in 2012 … and I am proud that she also happens to be my mum". Of course shivers ran through me and to think – on Mother's Day of all days.

I had the great pleasure of meeting Doris at her home along with her husband Tom and their daughter Sharon. Doris doesn't live in Valletta anymore however she grew up there so I figured there would be a good story to tell. I was asked to come to where the old salination plant was in Sliema near Tigné Point and Tom would take me upstairs. Once I arrived in their apartment, it became clear to me that the

Tignè Point from Valletta

story line was coming full circle – without having said more than a hello to Doris and her family. You see, the view through their expansive glass window is of Valletta – the money shot that everyone seeks from Sliema. I just about melted. "This was going to be interested", I thought to myself with raised eyebrows. I sat down with the family and began by getting to know everyone. Doris was beaming from ear to ear with a smile – eagerly waiting to tell her story. "I'm a Valletta girl", she proudly exclaimed.

Doris was born on 13 August 1946, one of ten children, on Merchant St in Valletta near the parish church of St Paul's Shipwreck. Her maiden name was Degiorgio and at the time of her birth, many of her family members had businesses on Merchant's Street. She was very proud to be a Valletta girl (still is). She used to boast about it when she lived in Valletta. There was nowhere else to go in those days for nightlife or fun daytime activities. The girls would parade up and down Republic Street with the boys standing and watching from the pavement. "There was no Facebook in those days," Sharon Cusens added. It would be around 4pm when the girls and boys went out. The girls had to be back home by 8:30pm. She was first introduced to Tom that way. "I chose him", she proclaimed. She was around 15 or 16. They had their own cliques, so to speak, in Valletta. Doris's friends would congregate in the Upper Barrakka Gardens.

Doris was a force to be reckoned with even in her early years. Sharon says that her mother is known as the 'Woman of Many Firsts'. Perhaps the most revealing evidence of rebellion was back in 1962. Doris and other Valletta girls were part of an all female football (soccer) team called the ICE Club whose premises were on South Street in Valletta. ICE apparently stood for Information, Culture and Entertainment - not referring to the much desired ice in the heat of the summer months. It was in Gżira at the old National Football Stadium where they played in the first female football match. Doris laughed as she recalled telling one of her teammates to kick the ball. That teammate inadvertently/ unknowingly kick the ball towards the wrong net. "We didn't really know the rules" she says. She recalled walking into school the

VALLETTA'S INTERNATIONAL APPEAL

Valletta from Marsamxetto

following Monday all stiff from the competition - only to be sent out of the class by her teacher. "Out, Doris!". Doris said she must have been told about seven times to get out. What Doris didn't know was that the Sunday newspaper had a picture of their match and apparently Doris was visible in it to the readers. "It was a scandal, taboo" she says. Even the nuns were upset with her.

When Tom and Doris got married, they moved to England for two years since Tom had been offered a position as an engineer. Before Doris left with Tom, she had been teaching physical fitness and education in schools. When she was pregnant with Simon in England, she attended prenatal classes. Noticing that Doris was a fit woman and an interest in it, the instructor asked her to assist with the class. Upon arriving back in Malta, Doris and Tom moved in with her mother in Valletta for six months. Because of her desire for fitness she decided to start fitness classes in Malta. Within a few years, she was putting together these fitness classes all over the island. Many men didn't like this since they thought a woman's place was in the home. As Tom puts it, "She caused a liberation of women". Because of her great contribution over the years with the 'Keep Fit' programme including having produced a fitness record album, she received the President's Award for her contribution to Maltese women. She ran many philanthropic fitness shows for many years. Adding to this, she started a fitness school for teachers - training the very first instructors in Malta.

Valletta A PERSONAL CITY GUIDE

She later brought instructors to London to showcase at the Royal Albert Hall in London. These were yet again growing pains for Malta in recognising the freedom of women. She was often threatened because of her drive to liberate women. That's quite an accomplishment for this Valletta girl.

They ended up buying a two-bedroom flat in Fgura – "I hated it," Doris interjected. "I cried my heart out day after day. I am a Valletta girl". The South was once perceived as being a less desirable place to live. Doris was the city girl and Tom the countryboy. Tom believes strongly that to remain grounded, one needs to be as close to nature as possible. For many years, Doris tried to convince Tom for them to move to Valletta, but Tom resisted – it wasn't going to happen.

Having felt that she had accomplished all that she wanted to do in fitness, she became a licenced tourist guide. She said she always wanted to be a guide. Her younger sister was one. Can you guess her most favourite place to guide in? Valletta, of course. She attracted many clients including VIPs such as Roger Moore – Mr Bond. More than the finer details taught at the university, she loved to tell stories of the places and people within Valletta; we are coming full circle with this piece. She received the award for top guide out of approximately eight hundred guides in 2012.

After some fifty years of marriage, that itch came back to Doris when she noticed during a walk that homes were being pulled down in Sliema to build a living complex. After viewing the plans of this building, Tom and Doris bought the flat knowing full well that the view would be of Valletta. "It was kind of a compromise after all these years", laughed Sharon. "That's my Valletta". When Doris lived in Valletta she had never really appreciated the look from across the Marsamxett Harbour.

As I said my thanks and goodbyes, I looked through that glass window and smiled. The Valletta girl had come full circle; Doris's appreciation of Valletta remains very grand.

Living in the City
INGRID EOMOIS

"What about Valletta?"

"Absolutely not. Who in their right mind would want to live there?"

Well, I would, actually. It was the year 2000 and after I had moved to Malta, my friends strongly advised me against living in Valletta. They warned me about the shabby properties and noisy neighbours. Between me and Valletta, however, even without the blessing of my friends, it was love at first sight. For some reason, I was always drawn to Malta's capital city – Il-Belt – as the locals call it: granted, it was slightly tainted and underrated, but nevertheless majestic and dignified.

As years went by, our cautious flirtation developed into a full-blown love affair. In the eighteen years since, I have witnessed the transformation of my beloved Valletta from a bleak, at times desolate place, to a vibrant, creative and stimulating city.

I imagine what Valletta must have looked like – and how different from today – towards the end of the 16th century, when it was built combining elements from Renaissance and Mannerist architecture. Born from the collaboration of two brilliant men: Francesco Laparelli, an Italian architect sent to Malta by the Pope himself, and his Maltese assistant, Ġilormu Cassar, who continued Laparelli's work after his mentor's departure. A city created by men for men, masculine energy in every yellowish stone. Resolute, straight streets, forming uncompromising right angles. Streets that, in summer, provide an enjoyable breeze but in winter can become ruthless wind tunnels.

Valletta A PERSONAL CITY GUIDE

Valletta today is like a distinguished gentleman, charming and enterprising in spite of his respectable age, touched-up here and there, albeit not always successfully.

16th century Valletta was characterised by stark, almost military architecture. It is understandable, since Malta's capital was built as a fortress to protect the Maltese islands from Ottoman invasion. In 1566, when Valletta's foundation stone was laid, the Great Siege was still fresh in the Knights' memory. The Great Siege is probably the single most important event in Maltese history. In 1565 about 30,000 Ottoman soldiers, on two hundred ships, invaded Malta, which was defended by a meagre army of between six and nine thousand, made up of knights, locals and slaves – truly a fight between David and Goliath. After a long siege lasting all summer, and including a number of devastating battles, Malta triumphed against all odds. The Order's French Grand Master, Jean de Valette, decided to erect a new city, on the practically devoid Sceberras peninsula that stood opposite Birgu, the Order's current stronghold. Obviously,

Typical balconies on West Street

the name of the new capital was derived from the name of its heroic, visionary founder.

From the 17th century onwards, owing to the growing popularity of baroque, Valletta gradually became the city we know today: extravagant and vain, theatrical façades, flamboyant works of art, overdecorated churches and palaces with high ceilings, next to which man seems minuscule and insignificant. We still get a glimpse of Mannerist Valletta when one knows where to look: for example, a number of buildings, including the Auberge d'Italie, have corners accentuated by rusticated quoins, a common feature in Mannerist architecture.

I finally made the move to Valletta in 2009, a fresh start in a quaint rented apartment, with a magnificent view over Grand Harbour. My new home is charming but small, and after a few years, yearning for more space, I started looking for a property I could call home. My partner, Paul, is born and bred in Valletta and does not need any persuasion. For both of us, Valletta is really the only place we would like to settle. While, after the war, many inhabitants of Valletta moved to other localities that offered modern and more comfortable accommodation, in more recent times, its appeal has increased dramatically. In 2017, Valletta is undoubtedly one of the most sought-after and costly areas in Malta to rent or purchase property. The avalanche of boutique hotels seems unstoppable.

Our real estate agent, a middle-aged man with wistful eyes and a soft smile, is kind and patient. He is indeed going to need patience and persistence since, in the coming months, we would be visiting countless (or so it seems) houses and flats.

One fine morning, we are meeting the agent in a street facing the sea. The day is still young, waves are lazily nibbling on worn rocks. The location is promising. After a massive, creaking door has been opened with an enormous key, we descend to the basement. In the dull light, reluctantly provided by a tiny light bulb, I remain initially speechless.

"So", says the agent, enthusiastically clapping his hands, "How do you like it? Location is fantastic and price is also affordable."

Valletta A PERSONAL CITY GUIDE

"I agree about the location but... but... where are the windows?", I hear myself stammering.

"Well, old houses in Valletta can be kind of dark..."

"...but this house has no windows! Not one! How is it possible to live here?"

We stand in a damp, mouldy crypt, which could only be described as a giant sarcophagus. Maybe once upon a time, this was a prison cell? I cannot imagine anyone but mice living here, and for these poor rodents I would feel nothing but pity.

"Well, in Valletta there is very little available," our agent apologetically said, continuing "and last week we did go to see that exquisite apartment near the monastery..."

"Fifth floor, no lift. Once I made it upstairs, I was already out of breath."

"But what about that property near the theatre?"

"Unfortunately, it is next to a kebab place, and it smelled like the meat was being cooked in the bedroom!"

Our agent was slowly giving up on us – who could blame him – and for a few weeks it was very quiet. Until, one afternoon, I hear his excited voice on the phone -

"Come quick, I have found you a house in St Nicholas Street! You have to see it before it gets dark because there is no electricity in the building."

A house with no electricity? Not very reassuring but intriguing nevertheless, so we leave work and rush to explore the new discovery.

The three-storey house is around four hundred years old, but its glory days are clearly in the past. For three decades, the building has been uninhabited, slowly and shamefully crumbling. The house belongs to one of Malta's noble families, who, quite irresponsibly, have abandoned it and it now lies huddled in a pile of rubble, like an injured animal. I tenderly stroke the cracked, centuries-old tiles, the mute witnesses of finer days.

"You don't deserve this", I whisper gently.

Our agent takes my muttering as a good sign, and continues with the tour. The house has five spacious rooms. In some rooms and in the internal yard, previous owners have clumsily built makeshift bathrooms, evidence of the fact that after the Second World War, at least three families lived here together.

LIVING IN THE CITY

The Second World War was an extremely difficult time for Malta. There were over 3300 air raids, more than 1500 dead civilians, and over 10,000 buildings damaged or destroyed completely, many of these in Valletta. In dire need of housing, many Maltese families lived in crammed conditions. Walking around in this splendid but sorrowful old house, I could only imagine how three large households managed to reside here, side by side.

We asked our agent to leave us the house keys, so that we could look around the building on our own. Dimming daylight is letting go for the night, and the house is almost completely dark. We move carefully from one room to another, stumbling on rubble, debris and discarded furniture. The house, like most old buildings in Valletta, has impressively-thick walls that keep it pleasantly cool during the scorching Maltese summer, and warm in the wet and humid winter. The walls, made of limestone, have been painted over and over again, the peeling paint revealing a distasteful rainbow.

In one of the rooms, we found a statue of the Virgin Mary holding a small lamp, hanging upside down. Statues of different

The refurbished Victorian market

Valletta A PERSONAL CITY GUIDE

saints, and crucifixes, used to be almost obligatory in every house in the past, and are still very common today. Who knows how long it has been hanging there? The Madonna's blue rope is dusty and chipped but she is still fervently holding on to a tiny bulb. We rescue the statue from its predicament, and place it gently on the floor to rest. The house is dark and damp, but it is unexpectedly pleasant and tranquil to squat on the dusty floor.

"Do you think that the house could be haunted?", I asked.

"Entirely possible," Paul shrugs his shoulders apprehensively, "Imagine everything that might have happened here in four hundred years!"

I agree. Moreover, locals always say that Valletta has plenty of haunted houses. Apparently, the ghost of Sir Oliver Starkey, de Vallette's private secretary, lives in what is now the Russian Cultural Centre in Merchants Street. Starkey, one of the closest friends of the legendary grand master, died in the middle of the 16th century when he was in his sixties. People who lived in the apartment on the top floor, often heard chatting and cutlery clinking as if there was a party nearby. At

St Barbara Bastion

night, they would feel cold breath on their faces, and hear furniture moving. Spooky!

We spotted a candle that still had some light left in it. It is rather exciting to exchange ghost stories by candlelight in an abandoned house. I asked Paul whether he knew the legend about the *ħares* (ghost) and when he told me that he did not, I was only too happy to repeat it.

"In Malta, we have a ghost story, repeating itself in different variations over many, many years – a story of the *ħares* –a ghost who visited Maltese housewives as an Ottoman soldier …"

"… and he visited only women? That sounds a bit suspicious!", chuckles Paul.

"You can laugh all you want, but it is said that the ghost only appeared when the husband was away, and would leave valuable presents – like money and jewellery - for the lady of the house."

"This just keeps getting better! Wouldn't it be nice if he came by our home as well?"

"Listen! If the wife somehow offended *il-ħares* or looked upon his gifts with contempt, then the next morning she would find dried leaves or dead insects instead of presents. When the ghost got really mad, he sometimes would also hit the ungrateful woman."

"Is that it? This is a strange story indeed."

"Wait, the punch line is still coming. Anthropologists think that with this legend, women often explained income that could not have been justified otherwise. Also, it provided a good excuse for having a black eye – instead of blaming a violent husband, they could accuse the ghost. It is very interesting that, the more independent women became, the less we hear stories of *il-ħares*. So, in a way, the incidence of this legend acts as an indicator of women's emancipation in Malta."

"That is interesting. But, in the meantime, what do you think of this house?"

"I think that we should buy it."

"Are you sure? It needs a lot of work."

"I don't think we will find anything more suitable. This is our house."

It is odd, how taking minor decisions can sometimes be lengthy and excruciating, while important decisions happen so swiftly and effortlessly. This does not mean, of course, that I have never regretted this spontaneous purchase.

After signing the papers, we were itching to start with the renovation works, stupidly and optimistically calculating that housewarming would take place in a year or so. Soon we would find out what it means to be a home-owner in a UNESCO-heritage city: not a single stone can be moved without the proper paperwork and permission. One and a half years later, the works had not yet started. Despair starts creeping in.

Gradually, though, light begins to flicker at the end of the tunnel. Magnificent, centuries-old walls emerge from under layers of paint. In one of the bedrooms, we discover a secret niche that could perhaps have been used as a hiding place by children who lived in this house. We saved as many old, hand-made Maltese tiles as we could, and gave them a new, dignified life. We restored the traditional Maltese balcony – *il-gallarija* – a perfect spot from which to watch the procession held annually for the feast of St Dominic. A cactus which I had never seen blooming, generously opens up its yellow flowers on our new roof terrace.

It would take us about three years to finally move in. Now I have accepted the fact that this old house will never be entirely ready – there is always something that needs to be done, or re-done. We still lack some furniture, there is stuff still in boxes, forgotten, and patiently waiting for a new chance. There will be the right time for everything, I keep repeating to myself.

However, I would not exchange my life in Valletta for anything.

Years ago, walking in the dark streets of Valletta I sometimes felt like I was the only living soul around. Now, there are buzzing wine bars and restaurants in every street. Cultural events are varied and vibrant – Valletta is truly ready for the title of the European Capital of Culture in 2018.

Our street, named after the church dedicated to St Nicholas, is a typical Valletta street filled with houses, all flaunting the stunning wooden balconies that first appeared in the capital in the 17th century and then spread all over the Island. The church was originally built as a Greek Orthodox church in the 16th century and was dedicated to St Nicholas of Bari, a fascinating saint who is at the centre of many

LIVING IN THE CITY

delightful legends. Looking up at the church entrance, one can see the statue of the Saint, portrayed holding three golden balls. According to popular legend, St Nicholas helped out a poor family with three daughters by giving them three bags of gold as dowry. He surely is a very busy saint, since his patronage includes children, sailors, fishermen, merchants, the falsely accused, brewers and many others! Today, unfortunately, this church is closed, although it is sometimes used by the Serbian Orthodox community.

Walking down the street, one can also notice religious statues and niches, prominent features in the Capital. The religious niches are usually built and cared for by local people. Statues were initially introduced by a German knight, Nesselrode, in the 18th century and illuminated by oil lamps that would light up the City. St Nicholas Street proudly boasts a statue of St Dominic, portrayed together with a torch-bearing dog. According to a bizarre legend, the Saint's mother, while pregnant, had a dream that her unborn baby was a dog. That must have been a real nightmare, rather than a dream! The church of St Dominic is nearby (our street is within its

Votive niche on St Nicholas Street

Valletta A PERSONAL CITY GUIDE

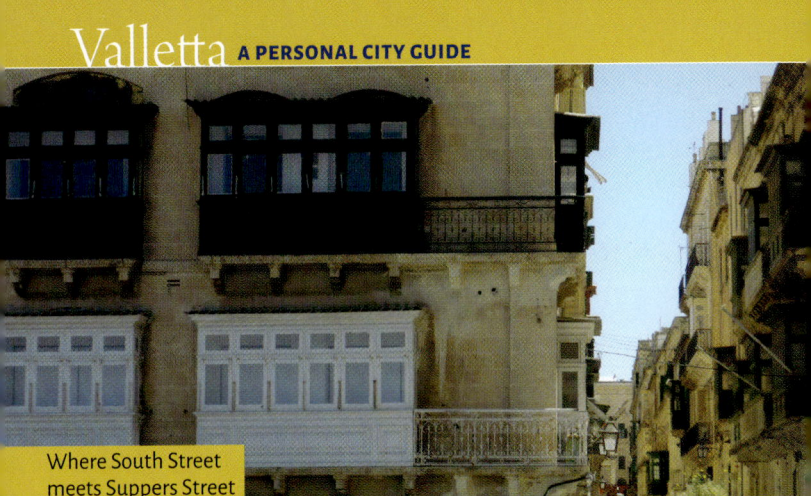

Where South Street meets Suppers Street

parish) and that also explains the niche of Our Lady of the Rosary, which is very close to our house. Devotion to this specific aspect of the Virgin Mary was introduced to Malta by the Dominican Order.

Twenty metres from our house, there is a bakery, and every night the baker places the round, fragrant loaves – the Maltese *ħobża* (plural – *ħobżiet*) – outside to cool. In the morning, on my way to work, the locals in front of a bar greet me with a slight nod, as if we belonged to the same secret society. Twice a week, Joe comes around with his van selling home-made *bigilla*, a Maltese dip made of mashed tic beans (known in Malta as '*ful ta' ġirba*' – Djerba Beans – these are similar to, but smaller than, broad beans, with a darker and harder skin), garlic, parsley and olive oil, with a generous helping of chilli flakes on the top for the brave.

Nearby young artists have opened a chic, upcycling studio. Just a few metres away, friendly hippies own a vegetarian café that offers the best smoothies in town. Our closest neighbour is Mario, who always has oily hands and smiling eyes, and whose garage-cum-workshop is a wonderland of nuts and bolts.

Traditional Valletta people are often loud, stubborn but genuine. They are fanatical about the local football team, Valletta F.C., and many of the men proudly help carry massive statues during the religious feasts of the many patron saints the city has. They also never shy away from a political argument. They are curious, warm and kind-hearted.

We are in good company.

Why Piano in a baroque city?

NARCY CALAMATTA

Valletta is a Baroque city both on the outside and on the inside. Baroque is not a style, but a manner of doing things. Baroque is not an orderly discipline but an orgy of ostentation. No one said, "As from today, all creative arts should be such". No, it just grew like a dirty habit.

In the 1973 TV documentary series, 'The Ascent of Man', Professor Jacob Bronowski speculates that the word 'Baroque' has its etymological roots in the Italian word '*baroccaio*', describing the rag-and-bone man who lived in a '*barracca*' or wooden-shed. The '*baroccaio*' would collect all sorts of items thrown away by the affluent, keeping them in his wooden-shed prior to loading them on his cart to go out to try to sell them.

Any artistic creation, be it architecture, music, performance or visual arts, that came after the Renaissance movement (circa 1585) and before Rococo (circa 1730) is deemed to belong to the Baroque period.

After the Knights of the Order of St John were chased out of the Island of Rhodes by the Turks, they set themselves up in Malta in 1530. The Turks followed them to Malta and laid siege on the Island in 1565, in what is now referred to as the Great Siege. The Knights and people of Malta resisted bravely and after the siege was lifted on 8 September 1565, and they had saved all of Europe from having to learn how to speak Turkish and converting to Islam, Pope Pius V made sure that Grand Master de Vallette received a lot of money as a reward from Christian Europe, and he brought to Malta the best Italian designer of military architecture of the

Valletta A PERSONAL CITY GUIDE

time, Francesco Laparelli. This enabled him to build a new fortified city which was eventually named after him – Valletta.

The Great Siege was a victory for the Catholic Church over the menacing and rising Ottoman empire, helping it to save face after having been vilified by the Protestant Reformation. This was for the Counter-Reformation Catholics to show that they were still powerful.

Catholic kings and princes became triumphant and ostentatious in their behaviour, and soon added so many decorations on the renaissance classicism that they left no space for more. In fact, in its own time this non-style was referred to as '*orror vacqui*' or 'the fear of leaving empty spaces'.

By 1572, only seven years after the Great Siege, the Knights had built bastions all around the peninsula known as Sceberras on the waterfront, and dug a moat on the fourth side which faced the hinterland. They had also built enough streets, palaces (auberges) and churches to accommodate the whole garrison and administration of the archipelago.

The Knights were a religious order, but also a military order. They liked the orderly style

Our Lady of Victory church

of Renaissance architecture. Basically it was a simple division of a façade into three vertical and three horizontal orders. The upright central section was the focal point of central perspective. It was the most important and imposing section where the central doorway (or an altar) was to be found and whatever elements you see on the left of it, are balanced exactly by what you see on its right side. The first buildings in Valletta were in fact very orderly.

This was the period when the Church in Rome was trying to become austere to appease Protestant criticism. Princes who were not however directly under its jurisdiction became more flamboyant, like Louis XVI of France, *Le Roi Soleil*.

By this time, the idea of over-decoration had already crept in all over Europe. However, the original Valletta buildings were kept sober to a degree. Subsequent grand masters ventured more towards the mundane and confirmed their power by adding further decoration. For example, just opposite the elegant small chapel of Our Lady of Victory, the City's first corner stone, we see another chapel built in classical style. This small church was built by the Italian Knights next to the Auberge d'Italie. If we look carefully, we notice that the canopy, or '*baldacchino*', over the main entrance had not been part of the original design but was added later.

Perhaps had they had more power in later years, they would even have covered it in marble and eventually put in inscriptions in gold. They could never have enough of decorations. The entrance to the Auberge d'Italie is clear proof of this as the Italian Grand Master, Fra Gregorio Caraffa, made sure history would not forget him by putting his bronze bust, surrounded by all sorts of symbols of power. Next corner down, there is the church dedicated to St Jacob. This was under the Bishop's jurisdiction and again shows the over-indulgence in showing off family connections and ecclesiastical high rank. Further down, along Merchants Street we find the Palace of Justice (*Castellania*). The marble decorations around the main entrance were clearly an eventual development. That was the Baroque manner, the more you have, the more you add.

Valletta A PERSONAL CITY GUIDE

So far we have seen some examples of over-decoration and ostentatious additions on the outside of buildings. The interiors of these same buildings confirm that the Knights of Malta tended to give vent to their pride by over-decorating, such as by covering everywhere in rich Carrara marble.

The Auberge de Castille (nowadays housing the Office of the Prime Minister of Malta) is a splendid edifice with an imposing façade which, dominating a wide expanse of land, rides over the bastions into the sky. Inside this palace, there is a magnificent double staircase flying in a clover-leaf on either side of the first central flight of stairs and embracing the stairwell at the top above the entrance, in a landing that leads to various chambers. A similar one is found in a palace in South Street which previously housed the Museum of Fine Arts after having served as the British admiral's headquarters.

What must be the most impressive interior in the whole of Europe is surely the nave that links the eight chapels of the Knight's conventual cathedral dedicated to their patron saint, St John the Baptist. This is indeed

Palazzo Castellania

the best example of *'orror vaqui'*. All the walls have bass-relief sculptures covered in gold leaf. In this magnificent interior, you will observe all the elements of visual arts, from a frescoed ceiling above, down marble pillars and along a floor decorated with hundreds of tombstones wrought in colourful marble *'intarsio'*, or marquetry in English. This floor was declared by UNESCO as being world heritage.

It took over 200 years to decorate the interior of St John's Cathedral. Therefore, it is understandable that we can trace the various developments from basic Renaissance to touches of Bernini's High Baroque and a hint of the subsequent Rococo, especially considering the omnipresent gold leaf embellishment.

The Knights of Malta wanted only the best. The greatest Baroque painter, Michelangelo Merisi da Caravaggio, left his most important works in their cathedral. Mattia Preti, *Il Calabrese*, painted the life story of St John on the ceiling as well as a number of other altar centrepieces.

It is wonderful to know that among a collection of extraordinary marble monumental sculptures, the central statuary group behind the main altar was designed by a Maltese sculptor, Melchiorré Gafa.

The Knights of Malta were ostentatious not only in the physical decorations but also in the musical area. They installed enough church organs to keep up with any other church in Europe, and in the *Bibliotheca* we find Monteverdi's compositions of Baroque music, written specifically for Malta. Some of them have still not been published. We also have Maltese composers' works of the time. The annual Baroque Music Festival, referred to elsewhere in this publication, invariably includes some newly published piece from this period, in a major concert with orchestra and choir in the floodlit interior of the Cathedral of St John.

During the reign of the Knights of St John on the Maltese Islands, between 1566 to 1798, Valletta, the new capital city of the island of Malta, in the middle of the Mediterranean, must have seemed like a tornado of Baroque Culture.

Previously we referred to the fact that Grand Master de Vallette

Valletta **A PERSONAL CITY GUIDE**

Main corridor of the Grand Master's Palace

brought to Malta the best Italian designer of military architecture. This was Francesco Laparelli, assistant to Michelangelo, who in 1566, was sent by the Pope to supervise the building of Valletta. He was a distinguished Military Architecture designer of the Baroque period and was the Pope's architect.

His plan was to surround the peninsula by a high defensive wall, serving as the deterrent that hindered the enemy who had to approach by boat. The weak underbelly of the City was the leeside, or the fourth wall facing the hinterland. Laparelli made sure that a deep moat was cut out of the mountain, and he built high bastions of Pharaonic proportions. The two plain, but imposing *'tenaie'* or pincer walls forming a double lateral defence of the entrance, are a pair of the most impressive bastions to be found anywhere in the world. (Malta and Gozo have over 40 kilometres of bastions, which surely is a wonder of man's achievement.)

Across this moat, Laparelli only left a narrow bridge that led through an adequate doorway built into the high wall, into the city. The idea was to make Valletta impregnable and keep the unwanted out.

Fast forward to the 21st-century and in 2015 a new wide-open entrance was inaugurated to make Valletta a more welcoming city. This breach in the fortification was the fruit of an idea by the veteran, world-renowned Italian architect, Renzo Piano. He had started his career with the iconic 'Pompidou Art Centre' in Paris which shows its intestines to all and sundry, and in more recent years designed the futuristic skyscraper known as 'The Shard' in London.

Most Maltese artists, myself included, at first resisted the engagement of Renzo Piano for this project. I fought the idea tooth and nail, when he was given the brief to build the new parliament building on the footprint of the old Royal Opera House, which still lay in ruins.

Eventually, Piano came out with a model for the new parliament building, which was too plain for the Maltese mentality nurtured on High Baroque. Contracts were signed and there was not much we artists could do about it.

When it was finally uncovered, we took a long time to get used to it. The proof of the pudding was

105

Valletta **A PERSONAL CITY GUIDE**

in the experience of living within it. I am a tourist guide, and I often take travel journalists around the new entrance to Valletta and the new structures and buildings immediately within. At first I had to be accompanied by a young Frenchman, Guillame Dreyfuss, an expert in architectural heritage, who explained to me the various implications. A bland ultra-modern building, if there is such a thing, was not easy for me to digest, especially in the light of the baroque wealth inside the City walls.

This young Frenchman, however, gave me the key of interpretation. Piano had used the same architectural idiom as Laparelli. He had managed to bring the plain, pharaonic bastions inside the City itself. The design included two useless wide staircases that go nowhere in particular on either side, creating a sense of space rather than the claustrophobic limitations of a fortress.

These stairs are in the same vernacular of Baroque military architecture, and similar ones can be found in other fortresses such as Fort Manoel on the small island in the middle of Marsamxett Harbour. Three hundred years

Renzo Piano's parliament building

WHY PIANO IN A BAROQUE CITY?

ago, they would have been used to give the possibility to a whole regiment of soldiers to move from one rampart to another within minutes.

Piano was impressed by the resilient quality of Maltese stone. He chose a particular quarry on the island of Gozo, and he commissioned the cutting of enormous blocks and large sheets of hard-stone to dress his new high bastions with.

He designed the parliament building in the form of two enormous blocks of stone floating in the air. He had observed how the elements corrode Maltese stone over the centuries, and inserted indentations in irregular patches to mimic the effect. We jokingly started calling it the cheesegrater at first. The hidden gaps are glazed, and allow a glimpse of the outside from inside but the sun never shines on these pseudo-windows. Buildings in Maltese stone are very difficult to keep cool if you let the sun in.

The two enormous flying blocks are not parallel, creating a sliver space through which you can see the original, high walls of St James Cavalier. You can easily observe the original, plain walls of the Baroque period of military

Valletta A PERSONAL CITY GUIDE

architecture within the entrance of the City.

The raised blocks of the new parliament building attain a lightness of being which gives them modernity. Piano ensured that the steel pillars underneath are surrounded by glass panes to indicate transparency of the goings-on. This is a metaphor in stone for our wish to have transparency in political activity. Piano had tricked us at first. Somehow, he knew that eventually we would come round to being proud of the new entrance to our capital city. Today, it has become a national meeting place with adequate shelter from the sun and the occasional rain. We have become used to expecting to enjoy formal or informal events on the stairs or in the open space including high fashion, concerts and even theatre. One such event was when on the 2015 UNESCO World Day for *Commedia dell'Arte*, I took my troupe to perform my play, 'Love Potion for Arlecchino', on one of the staircases flanking the building. Arlecchino is a stock comic character, universally adopted in the 17th Century known for its High Baroque Culture. *Commedia dell'Arte* was popular in Malta then. It is still popular now. The success of that event amply showed that Piano had managed to use the architectural vernacular of the grand period of the Knights so far in the past, to erect a building designed for the modern day and for the future.

The Maltese *dgħajsa tal-pass* was the means by which Royal Navy sailors made their way to shore and to the pleasures that Valletta had to offer. A shore-pass was needed, and the boatmen would insist on seeing it. They shouted demand "pass, pass" gave the *dgħajsa* its nickname. The popularity with sailors earned this boat's name the pride of a place in the *Oxford English Dictionary*.

dghaisa ('daɪsə). Also **dghajsa**, **dhiassa**. [Maltese.] A boat resembling a gondola, used in Malta.

1893 'S. Grand' *Heavenly Twins* I. ii. 214 A rainbow fleet of dghaisas...propelled by oarsmen who stood to their work. 1923 *Blackw. Mag.* Dec. 744/2 Not my business the dghaisas skated about the surface of the harbour. 1940 M. Dickens *Mariana* ix. 339 Wireless messages from Aunt Annabelle telling them to jump into a *dhaisa* and come ashore. 1964 *House & Garden* Dec. 28/1 The Maltese dghajsa...is first cousin to the gondola of Venice.

dgiahour, obs. form of GIAOUR.

The smells of the City

VERONICA BARBARA

When we travel, our senses somehow seem to become more powerful and they manage to absorb so much more of the surroundings than they normally do for us. Whereas in our hometown, we might never really take much notice of the church bells tolling or of the sweet perfume of flowers from a front garden, when in a foreign country these little details are picked up more predominantly by our senses, creating the loveliest memories and the most unforgettable experiences. Out of all the senses, I think that the sense of smell is possibly the one that brings us closer to our travel memories.

All cities have their particular scents and Valletta is no exception. Situated on a peninsula and always enjoying a breeze, the smell of the sea is perhaps the most dominant of all, bringing a tinge of freshness to a busy and cosmopolitan space. It's almost as if this smell wants to remind visitors of the importance of the Grand Harbour to the Maltese people.

The numerous shops along the city's hectic streets all contribute their own particular scent. Soap outlets usually exude a whiff of citrus, lavender and jasmine. Artisans' shops are characterised by the sharp smell of freshly-carved wood, while sweetshops, especially Camilleri's on Merchants Street, make you forget whatever diet you had just embarked upon, so enticing is the smell of the various candy and sweet pastries on display.

Valletta is also a city of restaurants and cafeterias, each with its own character, atmosphere and, of course, menu! My appetite is always awakened whenever I pass in front of a typical Maltese restaurant, and the individual or combined smells of rabbit stew, meat *braġjoli* or fish in tomato sauce hit my nostrils. These three dishes are perhaps the most traditional main courses among the locals, usually reserved for the day of the village feast, or some other special family occasion.

During a morning excursion to Valletta, whether for shopping or sightseeing, rabbit stew might be a bit too much however. Locals would probably opt for a typical *ftira biż-żejt*, a kind of flattened round bread, similar to an Italian *ciabatta*, spread thickly with tomato paste (*kunserva*) and olive oil, and filled with onions, capers, olives and possibly Maltese sausage, tuna or *ġbejniet* – Maltese sheep's milk cheeselets. Otherwise, if you decide not to be so health conscious for a day, you might indulge in the traditional *pastizzi*, the smell of which will immediately make you feel hungry. These snacks are puff pastry envelopes generally filled with either *ricotta* or mushed peas. If on the Maltese Islands during Holy Week, make sure you ask for the seasonal anchovy *qassatat*. They are simply delicious!

Of course, for those who do not wish to be so adventurous with local cuisine, there is a whole

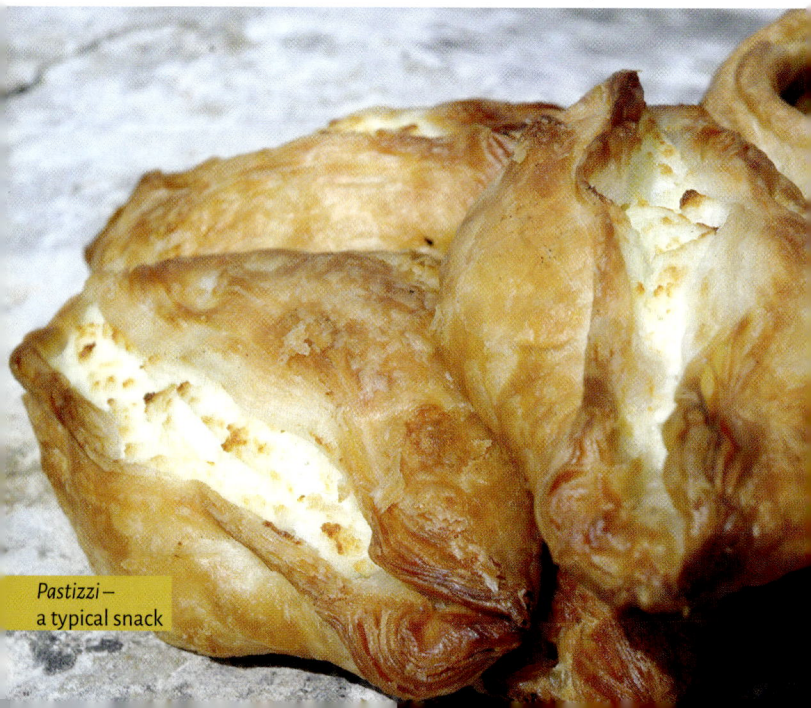

Pastizzi – a typical snack

THE SMELLS OF THE CITY

variety of other cuisines to opt for. Be it the smell of sweet and sour sauce from a Chinese take-away, lamb *shish* from a Turkish kebab house, oven-baked pizza from an Italian pizzeria, quinoa salad from the vegetarian restaurants, or a traditional fried English breakfast from British style cafeterias, Valletta has it all. This mix of food and smells is, in a way, another expression of the international culture created by the people who have built, ruled, inhabited and given a part of themselves to this special city over the centuries.

You might not be much of a food person but in Malta you cannot make do without drinking a lot of liquids, especially between June and September when the weather is extremely hot by normal European standards, sometimes even hitting and going higher than 40 degrees Celsius at the height of summer. And, once again, Valletta does not disappoint. First choice for all Maltese is Kinnie, a local soft drink made with bitter oranges. Served cold, with a wedge of orange or lemon, its bitter-sweet taste is instantly refreshing, with it now being produced in a variety of flavours.

For those who prefer something more natural, what could be more

Inside Caffe Cordina

Valletta **A PERSONAL CITY GUIDE**

satisfying than a glass of freshly-squeezed orange juice? A tree well known in the Mediterranean as from classical times, the orange tree was at first cultivated not for its fruit, but rather for its beauty in gardens and for the lovely scent and vision of orange blossoms. Professor Alain Blondy (2003: 8) explains how an essential oil extracted from orange blossoms was used in the production of perfume and was an important element in Maltese trade. Blondy also adds that in the 18th century, the Portuguese Grand Masters of the Order of St John introduced the 'red Portuguese' variety to the Maltese Islands, a sweet fruit available all year round, which soon became extremely popular for its refreshing taste. Nowadays different varieties are available coming from all over the globe. There are still a small number of lucky families that have the luxury of enjoying their very own Maltese oranges available in their own gardens.

Early morning in Valletta? The predominant smell will definitely be that of coffee. Those working in Valletta, more often than not, start their day with a quick cup of freshly-brewed coffee to kick-start their day.

Honey-rings – typical Maltese sweet

THE SMELLS OF THE CITY

Otherwise the second option is tea with milk and sugar, another Maltese favourite inherited from our colonial history. It is very common to find the old-school corner cafeterias serving tea with milk in glasses (not cups), with the obligatory two *pastizzi* on a side-plate, to their regular elderly customers who congregate in their habitual groupings on a daily basis to discuss local happenings, especially sport and politics.

Evenings in Valletta are characterised by music, the rustling of leaves as birds call it a day, and the sound of cruise liners exiting the harbour after an eventful day for their passengers. The perfect atmosphere, in other words, for a romantic stroll or a dinner with friends and family. And how can a dinner be complete without a glass of wine, or two?

Wines are always welcome but it is a fact that, especially in summer, Maltese people love most their glass, or two of beer. The smell of beer is part and parcel of any festivity, be it a cultural festival, a traditional *festa*, a political or sport celebration, or even just a get-together between friends. Farsons Group own and manage the main brewery on the

A popular eatery in Valletta

Valletta A PERSONAL CITY GUIDE

Bistros and wine bars along the streets of Valletta

Maltese Islands, and produce Cisk Lager, undoubtedly the most popular beer on the Islands, now also sought-after worldwide.

To share the Maltese experience to the full, make sure you spend some time with the jovial locals, tasting the multicultural cuisine of the Islands and toasting to the beauty of Valletta. Cheers, and enjoy your stay!

References:
Blondy A. (2003) A treasure of 18th century Malta: The Maltese Orange. *Treasures of Malta*, X:1, 7-11.

Teatru Manoel

NARCY CALAMATTA

Walking down Republic Street, the main street of Valletta, you get to St George's Square outside the Grand Masters' Palace. There you turn left and walk down the gentle slope along Old Theatre Street. The British called it that because for them the 'new' theatre was the one they had built in 1866 that was subsequently destroyed by enemy action in 1942.

The Maltese call the street *Triq it-Teatru*. *Triq* is the Maltese word for street and *Teatru* is a Sicilian dialectical corruption of the Latin/Italian word for theatre, *'teatro'*. This means that for the Maltese the culture of dramatic art predates the British influence, since the 'old' is not present.

Italian influence

The building of the Manoel Theatre was commissioned by the Portuguese Grand Master Antoine Manuel de Vilhena in 1731 and opened the following year with a production of an Italian free-verse drama based on the Greek mythological tragedy, *La Merope*, by Shipione Maffei. Once the first production at the 'Teatro Pubblico' was an Italian tragedy, then we can easily conclude that Italian was of major

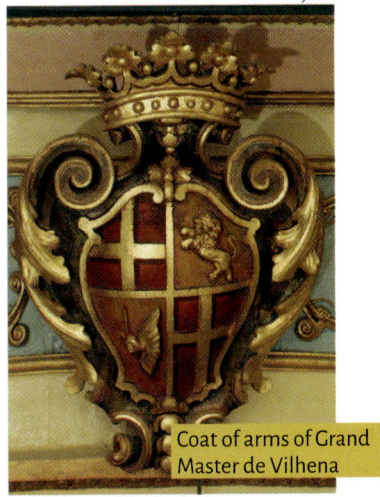

Coat of arms of Grand Master de Vilhena

Valletta A PERSONAL CITY GUIDE

cultural influence even under a Portuguese Grand Master. Why was it so?

Of the eight 'Langues' (languages) or regiments of the Holy Order of St John (Knights of Malta), the one from an Italian princedom had brought with it all the culture of the Italian High Renaissance in 1530. The best military architects, painters and scenographers came from Italy.

When Valletta was built, and the Knights started to live in it around 1572, they eventually built their official residences in the form of big palaces, which they called *Auberges*, in French.

The Auberge d'Italie is still standing in the top end of Merchants Street. It will soon open as our new Museum of Fine Arts for the occasion of Valletta being the *European Capital of Culture 2018*. Then the public will be able to admire its large halls which were once used for theatrical performances.

The first such performance recorded at the Auberge d'Italie was held in 1631. You can imagine how these bachelor, rich and idle knights enjoyed performing texts based on classical myths. Keep in mind that they also portrayed the female character parts. This

The stage-curtain and stalls of the Theatre

theatrical activity became very popular among the knights of various 'langues' and their guests.

Maltese aristocracy

They would also invite families of the Maltese nobility, descendants of the medieval Sicilian aristocrats. The marquises, dukes and barons cherished the opportunity of making grand entrances at the Auberge d'Italie, accompanied by their wives and young daughters in all their fineries. Italian theatrical performances were occasions for ostentation and sophistication.

We have records showing the presence of an Italian foreign company performing at the Auberge d'Italie in 1660. Thirty seven years later, a group of Maltese actors were also performing there, undoubtedly in the Italian language.

Honest princely heritage

The practice of high culture events, contemporarily with the great kingdoms of Europe, gave the Knights a sense of power. Small wonder then, that when Grand Master Vilhena wanted to leave yet another edifice to be remembered by, he built the Manoel Theatre, which he named *Teatro Pubblico* (a theatre for the general public). You can easily conclude that the word 'public' was not meant to include hawkers, fishermen and farmers, but the elite class from the former capital city of Mdina and its suburb, Rabat. Rich merchants and galley-owners, from the first fortress by the sea occupied by the sea-faring knights, Birgu (Vittoriosa) and eventually from the rest of the Three Cities, were also invited to share in this sophistication of theatrical performances.

Honest entertainment

The original inscription in Latin still in place above the main door reads, *AD HONESTAM POPULI OBLECTATIONEM* (For the honest recreation of the people). The word 'honest' should indicate that there was an alternative (not so honest) distraction a couple of streets up, which the younger knights were forbidden to frequent by an edict (1578) of Grand Master Le Cassier who had built St John's Cathedral.

By building the *Teatro Pubblico*, the Portuguese Grand Master Vilhena made sure he usurped the monopoly till then enjoyed by the Italian Knights.

Valletta A PERSONAL CITY GUIDE

TEATRU MANOEL

Bijou jewel box

The architect relied on the well-accepted design of the Teatro Massimo in Palermo. Considering Malta had previously formed part of the reign of the Two Sicilies (Napoli and Palermo), this new theatre was quite a come-uppance. The original design was a semi-circular pit (in Greek, the orchestra) surrounded by tiers of boxes.

At first it looked quite austere, reflecting the seriousness of the religious order of the Knights of St John. Subsequent Grand Masters decorated every detail in the auditorium in the ostentatious, gilded Baroque fashion. It is today a bijou of interior decoration, quite like a jewel box.

I am the State

De Vilhena was not the only one with airs of grandeur. In 1741, only nine years after the theatre opened its doors, a new Grand Master, Manuel Pinto de Fonseca, wanted to celebrate his election grandly. He asked for a performance to be enacted in his honour and bought all the seats himself to distribute among family and friends.

This grandiose gesture was one that was also used much more recently by Donald Trump in his election campaign, when he booked all the seats of a cinema and gave them away for free. The cinema was showing the film 13 Hours that vilified Hilary Clinton for her losing a US ambassador in Libya when she was Secretary of State. Incidentally that film was entirely filmed in Malta. Two years later, Grand Master Pinto initiated a practice of contracting a private theatre impresario to organise the season of theatrical events. Pinto fancied himself as a supreme sovereign, and he was wont to express his power even at the theatre, especially by making sure to exclusively occupy the purposely-built central 'royal box' in the first tier. Those days, the Grand Masters of the Order of St John wanted the world to know that they alone, and not the people, were the state.

Nicolò: a Maltese genius

The Maltese people come from the original melting pot of nations, which is Valletta's Grand Harbour. One of these was the founder of the French-origin family, Isouard. Their prodigious son, Nicolò, had already composed an opera and had it performed at the Teatru Manoel in 1791. It was a comic opera based on Italian *Commedia dell'Arte* characters and was called *Casaciello Perseguitato da un Mago* (He obviously still had a lot of French blood in him because eight years later, when the French under Napoleon Bonaparte took over Malta from the Knights of St John, he was made impresario at the Manoel Theatre). Soon after, he was asked to go and work at the *Operà de Paris* where he had great success with his *opera bouffe*. Today, you can still see his bust on the right flank of the building, with the inscription – Nicolò de Malte.

Pardonne moi
In 1798, Napoleon kicked out Grand Master von Hompesch and his Holy Order of Knights quite unceremoniously, and seven days later went off to start the battle of the Nile. The Maltese church leaders and the nobility urged the peasants to revolt, and General Masson, with his French garrison, locked all the entrances to the impregnable Valletta city. He threw out all the uncooperative Maltese, and waited for help while

General view from the stage

outside Valletta, the revolution was raging.

The Maltese leaders asked King George III of England for help, and he sent Admiral Horatio Nelson to set up a blockade around Malta, using the British fleet.

One night, General Masson organised a show at the Manoel Theatre to celebrate a Napoleonic victory. After the show, late at night, some French army officers coming out of the Theatre, noticed some burning torches bobbing up and down in the harbour on Valetta's west side. They sent a patrol to investigate, and caught a group of Maltese resistance fighters sneaking in their fellow fighters through a tunnel below the sheer bastion at the water's edge.

The next day the insurgents were arraigned in the main square (today St George's Square), and along with their leader, a priest by the name of Dun Mikiel Xerri, were summarily executed by a firing-squad.

Had there been no show at the Manoel the night before, history could have been much different. After 18 months, the starved French garrison abandoned Malta and the Maltese leaders asked the British to move in as protectors.

Military theatre fans

The British declared Malta as their colony in 1813. They exploited the well-protected harbours to accommodate their formidable fleet. Hundreds of thousands of sailors and soldiers were residing in Malta or on ships harbouring here. Thousands of officers needed to have entertainment away from where the lower rank sailors and soldiers could go.

The most elite form of entertainment was Italian lyric opera at the now renamed 'Royal Theatre' (Manoel). You can imagine the hundreds of officers in their high regalia and ceremonial uniforms, accompanied by their lady wives wearing sophisticated gowns and tiaras, indulging in cherishing the best performances Europe could offer.

The Manoel expands

Soon they decided to enlarge the Theatre, and pushed back the stage to fit in eight new boxes at the proscenium arch. They raised the roof and built a higher balcony to bring the capacity to around six hundred, the capacity it still has today. Even so, the increase of seats made theatre more popular among the *bon ton* and, in 1866, they inaugurated a brand new theatre, the Royal Opera House, seating 1,200 patrons at the entrance to Valletta. Along with Italian opera, they invited English production companies from Covent Garden in London to stage Shakespeare plays there.

The bad times

The Manoel lost its 'royal' appellation and fell into disrepute. With the turn of the century, it was converted into a cinema, and when bigger and grander cinemas were built in the Valletta main street, the Manoel closed. During World War II, it was used as an emergency doss house, where sailors who lost the last transport to their ship would spend the night lying on the floor in the theatre boxes, paying a few pennies for a night.

In the early 50s, still in private hands, it was revived to house itinerant opera companies fully subsidised by the Italian government, which put on respectable opera seasons of more than eight different operas each year.

The re-birth of the Manoel

In 1955, the Maltese government recouped the ownership of the Theatre and started a refurbishment programme. When the theatre was properly restored to its former glory in 1961, a varied bill of British theatre performances was inaugurated. Although the English influence was strong, Maltese theatre companies, such as Maleth, started presenting their translations from Italian classics in the newly-named Manoel Theatre.

Soon some Maltese play-wrights started cropping up. However, the more successful ones followed the trends of the London West End fare. Maleth started translating American comedies by Neil Simon and gradually, the Maltese theatre audience's mentality became more and more Anglo-Saxon.

An English amateur drama company, which had been set up 50 years earlier exclusively for British officers and their wives, started accepting Maltese actors in its ranks after the 1964 Independence. By the time the British forces and influential imperial corporations had completely left Malta in 1979, the theatre mentality of the Maltese was moulded in the British norm of a middle-class pastime for middle-class entertainment.

Maltese identity

In the 70s, the Manoel was the National Theatre of Malta. Anywhere else was considered provincial and populist. The Maltese government instituted the first-ever National School of Music, sponsored by the Austrian government. The remnants of the British Admiral's chamber orchestra were set up as an embryonic national orchestra, under the umbrella of the Manoel Theatre organisation. Today, it has become an internationally-recognised and acclaimed philharmonic orchestra.

With the help of the British Council, the government also instituted the first ever drama school as part of the Manoel Theatre organisation. Maltese play-wrights started having regular engagements to write about various Maltese historical political incidents, and going to the Manoel to see a play in Maltese became acceptable social behaviour.

Maltese opera singers like Miriam Gauci started building a name for themselves on the international circuit. A few actors, who had first found their feet on the Manoel boards, took a short cut to Hollywood, such as Jon

Main door of the Theatre

healthy number of purely Maltese drama productions. However the majority of shows in the Manoel's calendar are still foreign and mostly Anglo-Saxon.

Healthy cultural theatre seasons

Teatru Manoel has once again become home to visiting foreign spectacles of opera and classical ballet. It also organises an annual festival of Baroque music, with the participation of top choirs and orchestras from all over Europe. Junkets of patrons come out to Malta specifically to enjoy this one-week festival. In its repertoire, it includes compositions of the epoque by Maltese composers, and some unpublished scores young Maltese have a craze for London West End style stage musicals, and closely-guarded franchises have been allowed to be produced locally by the Maltese.

The visitor to the Theatre in the winter season is guaranteed a weekly classical musical concert of international standard , possibly with visiting celebrity performers. With some previously-researched bookings, one could also attend high-calibre performances of stage musicals, with local stars performing.

Many an international celebrity likes to vaunt in her/his CV a performance at Teatru Manoel. It has a great history and is one of the oldest theatres still active in Europe.

Valletta
A PERSONAL CITY GUIDE

Allegory of Victory, carved stone at St John's Co-Cathedral

The most beautiful floor in the world

DANE MUNRO

St John's Co-Cathedral at Valletta, Malta is regarded as the pearl of Baroque of the Mediterranean. Few churches can compete with its quantity and quality of mesmerising art. It was originally built as the conventual church of the Military and Hospitaller Order of St John of Jerusalem, Rhodes and Malta, also known as the Knights of the Order of Malta. One needs to understand the art at St John's also from the point of view of the identity of the Order, whose self-appointed task was to patrol the Mediterranean Sea to protect the Maltese islands and Christian shipping from North African and Ottoman pirates and slave traders attacks and to free Maltese and other Christian slaves from a miserable existence in North Africa and in Turkey.

A new city after the devastation of the Great Siege

The Order and the people of Malta had barely survived the Great Siege of 1565, a three and a half month siege of Malta by the Ottomans. Emperor and Sultan Suleiman the Great had thought that he could conquer the islands of Malta within one week and thus use them as a stepping-stone to expand his Empire to the west, that is, Spain and southern Europe. Fortunately, tiny Malta proved to be a stumbling block and was hailed as the Shield of Europe. The victory of the Order and its survival, in the Great Siege had brought it immense popularity throughout Europe. Consequently, the Order's victory was interpreted as the triumph of the Catholic faith over Islam. It made the Order's treasury and ranks swell, as many aristocratic families offered landed property

Valletta A PERSONAL CITY GUIDE

and monetary gifts and, more importantly, their children as novices to the Order. Having their sons as potential heroes greatly enhanced the status of aristocratic families amongst their peers.

After so many of the population and knights of Malta had been killed and so many buildings destroyed, a new capital city was planned. This new city was named after Grand Master Jean Parisot de Valette, the man who had led the Order and the Maltese through the Great Siege of 1565. Impregnable and unscalable walls were built around the peninsula of Sceberras, and one may say that these walls are an embodiment of fear, fear of the Ottomans. Should they return, however, the Ottomans would find a city ready for them. Thanks to a different opinion of the successor of Süleyman, the Ottomans concentrated more on the Balkans than on the Mediterranean.

Grand Master de Valette laid the first stone of the new city on 28 March 1566, at the first church of Valletta, the church of Our Lady of Victories, showing gratitude to Our Lady for helping the Maltese and Knights not only to survive the Great Siege but also to win this incredible battle. On

The Great Siege of 1565

his death in 1568, de Valette was buried in the crypt of this church.

St John's Conventual Church

Valletta, within its walls, was being filled with official buildings for the Order, churches and homes. Grand Master Jean de la Cassière decided on a new conventual church for the Order in Valletta. Conventual, because wherever the Order had their most important institutions, such as the navy, treasury, library and other government buildings, they called this the *convent*, as they lived and worked there together as Religious (men).

This new conventual church was not planned as an extravagant and jubilant church, as it would become in later times. Then there was simply too much mourning about the loss of life caused by the Great Siege. More crucially, war and sieges cost money, and the Order's treasury was rather empty after the Great Siege.

The importance of the Great Siege as a benchmark against which heroism and triumph could be measured cannot be underestimated. The Order emphasised its privileged role, both as the protector of the faith and as God's protégé. An

Allegory of Victory of the Order

inscription on the Couvre Port, a fortification in Vittoriosa, Malta, reads: *DOMINE OBUMBRASTI SUPER CAPUT MEUM IN DIE BELLI* (O Lord, you have covered my head in the day of war). Such an inscription is a key to understanding the Order's perception of its place in this world. As the inscription suggests, in the opinion of the Order, God had saved Malta from a total annihilation by the Ottomans. That was certainly the understanding of Grand Master Jean de Valette (ruled 1557-68).

De la Cassière placed the first stone of the new conventual church in 1571 and the church was consecrated in 1577. Grand Masters who had been buried elsewhere were brought together in a crypt beneath the main altar of the new St John's conventual church. A splendid sepulchral monument of Grand Master de Valette, hero of the Great Siege, was created, and the inscribed text narrates his piety and prowess.

> ...when in the Year of the Lord 1565 he freed Malta from the siege of Süleyman..., saving the old city of Mdina and the fortresses of St Angelo and St Michael, chasing the Turks from the whole island and swept clean each side of this sea of pirates, and constructed the new city of Valletta, extremely safe against the enemies of our Faith, a bulwark and eternal monument of de Valette... he was a terror to the enemy, dear to his own, whence not without reason, he was called the guardian-of-the-people and the curse-of-the-enemy by everyone. He was the dread of Asia and Libya and once the Shield of Europe, after he had subdued the Turks by means of his Sacred Arms. He was the first to be buried in this propitious city which he founded. Here lies de Valette, worthy by eternal honour.

During the building of the new capital city of Malta, Valletta, the designer of the church, the Maltese military engineer and architect Gerolamo Cassar, created a simple façade, resembling the fortification walls of the new city of Valletta. And it remained simple until Baroque arrived in the 1630s. Since then, the exterior of the church no longer reveals what lies behind it. Exuberant Baroque is probably insufficient to describe the church's concept of total art. Another binding element is the patron of the Order, St John the Baptist. His life is painted in oil on the barrel vault of the church

THE MOST BEAUTIFUL FLOOR IN THE WORLD

by the Calabrian artist Mattia Preti, who used the Gospel of St Matthew for the sequencing. Many other artists of name have contributed to the church, such as the painter Caravaggio, the sculptor Ciro Ferri, artworks by the school of Bernini and many others. Just to give one example, when the Aragonese noble man Ramon Perellos y Roccaful became Grand Master in 1697, he bestowed a set of Flemish tapestries to the church, many of them by the design of Peter Paul Rubens.

Within the nave at St John's, there are four passages and eight chapels, belonging to each of the eight langues (or nationality sections of the Order), namely Auvergne, Provence, France, Aragon, Castille and Portugal, Italy, Bavaria (Germany), and England (with Scotland and Ireland).

It is actually the two Aragonese brothers of the Cotoner family who financed the big push forward into Baroque. First Raphael, then Nicola Cotoner became Grand Masters of the Order, between 1660 and 1680, spending large sums of their private money to embellish the interior of the church. The

St John's Co-Cathedral

Valletta A PERSONAL CITY GUIDE

Interior view of the Co-Cathedral

THE MOST BEAUTIFUL FLOOR IN THE WORLD

Valletta A PERSONAL CITY GUIDE

sepulchral monument of Nicola Cotoner is a very prominent one, full of symbolism and political and military elements.

The Floor of Floors

St John's Co-Cathedral has indisputably the most beautiful floor in the world. The Order was at its outset a product of Europe's medieval feudal society and during these times, structures of close-knit kinship gave rise to the development of the nobility of the robe and of the sword and the notion of Christian Chivalry. Military prowess and honour became of major importance. Also, the display of wealth had great importance. Such notions too are found in the eulogies of the deceased Knights inscribed in marble at St John's Co-Cathedral. The memorial floor of marble polychrome intarsia (marble inlaid) slabs is a major defining characteristic, and their public display forms part of the collective identity of the Knights of Order of St John, showing the solidarity between the living and the dead Knights. The inscribed eulogies always bear an educational and inspirational intent, whose validity would serve as a witness of immortality and mould the mind of any Knight or passer-by. Many knights, especially novices, would come to the church and read aloud the texts of these exemplary members of the Order of St John, in order to learn, to emulate and to wonder about their lives and death. Through the messages on the slabs and monuments, both in inscribed text and iconography, the memory of the Order was ensured, serving the justification of its *raison d'être*.

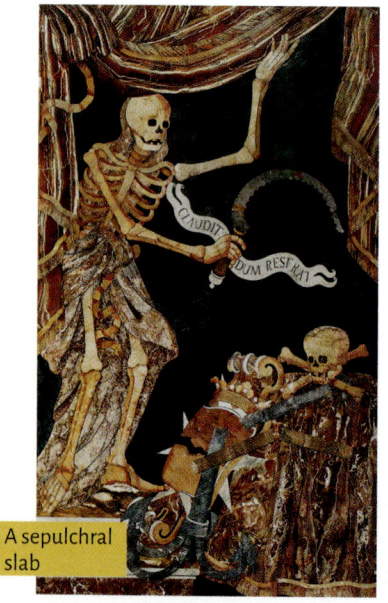

Sepulchral slabs are to be found all over the church floors, most of them written in Neo-Latin. Most of the 400 sepulchral slabs and monuments contain polychrome

A sepulchral slab

intarsia workmanship. In case of a slab, the basic material is always a plate of Carrera marble, soft and easy to work with. This is chiselled out to a depth of about 5 to 10 smm and laid in with slices of coloured marble. Afterwards, the surface is polished until it is seamless and smooth. On average, a slab weighs about 1000 kg. These slabs were then engraved with a text, often made years before the person in question actually died. These sepulchral slabs are made to walk over, as this was regarded one of the highest forms of humility. This may surprise visitors, but the slabs are indeed made to walk over, stand on, contemplate, pray for the reprisal of the deceased knight's soul. In this respect, the slabs of the floor work together with the magnificent paintings on the barrel vault by the aforementioned artist Mattia Preti. This barrel vault ceiling is meant as an optical illusion, allowing the living to look straight into Heaven. In the middle section one may see God in Heaven. On the sides, adjacent to the windows, there are the saints and holy men and women of the Order, who act as intermediaries between the deceased and God, as patron-saints are wont to do. Therefore, the living may stand on a tombstone, and engage in a mutual understanding with the deceased. I may stand on your tombstone and I acknowledge that this is the greatest form of humility. I may enjoy the art, symbols and iconography of your slab and will read your inscribed text and will strive to emulate your example. I, as my thanks for this all, will look up to God in Heaven and the patron-saints and make my prayer for your soul so that you may arrive in Heaven, after your soul has been cleansed of sin in Purgatory. Sin? Yes, chivalry and knighthood carry an

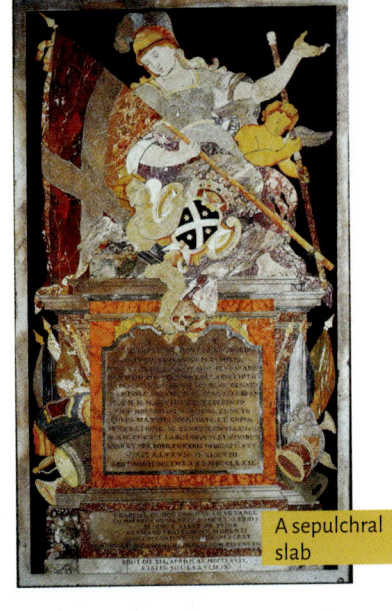

A sepulchral slab

Valletta A PERSONAL CITY GUIDE

intrinsic form of sin, incorporated in the violence a knight carries out to fulfil his duties. When a knight dies during an engagement with the enemy in a just war, he was regarded as a martyr and it was believed that his soul would go straight to Heaven. Standing on a tombstone is therefore not scary or disrespectful; in the past it had a function of which most visitors are unaware of, until now.

This extraordinary collection of commemorative slabs owes its existence to the Order of St John and, like many other church floors, it has developed and changed over the centuries. Slabs were added and removed or repaired when worn, but many were also subjected to a total make-over. Even the configuration of the floor itself was changed over time, sometimes drastically and on a large scale. St John's was also the Order's *aula heroum* or hall of fame, a place which grew from humble beginnings into a

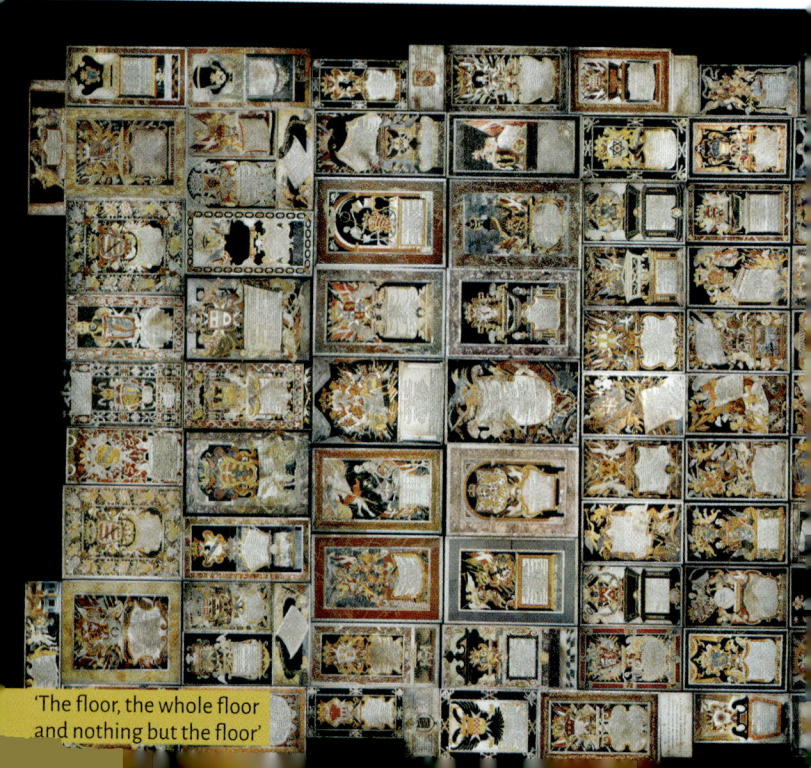

'The floor, the whole floor and nothing but the floor'

THE MOST BEAUTIFUL FLOOR IN THE WORLD

showcase of the High Baroque in Malta. The church and its floor have undergone consecutive stages of artistic developments, of which Mannerism and the Baroque have had the greatest impact. These artistic styles were first developed in Sicily and Italy. From the seventeenth century onwards, they were also produced in Malta, since the quality of the local craftsman (*marmisti*) was excellent and there was no shortage of raw materials. Most of the tombstones were organised through notaries, who contracted *marmisti* and laid out the costs, remuneration and duration of the work. Obviously, everything had to adhere to the Order's ethos and pathos, and there were various 'approved' designs in inscribed texts and iconography to remind passers-by to emulate the exemplary lives of those commemorated.

This public display to the memory of deceased heroes

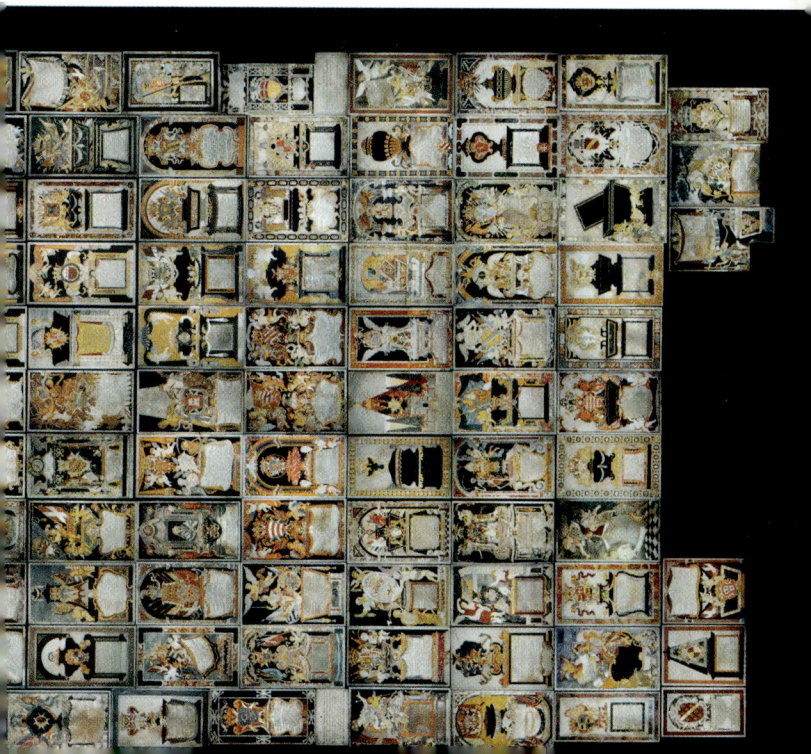

Valletta A PERSONAL CITY GUIDE

and defenders of the Catholic faith initiated competition between *langues* to create the most beautiful chapel that their money and influence could buy. Also, on a different scale, it is not unthinkable that the Order tried to vie with the churches of Rome. A trend thus ensued to obtain eye-catching slabs prompting intercessory prayers for their souls.

To some extent, the floor slabs at St John's have lost their original meaning. Apart from some exceptions, the floor slabs are much less the object of intercessory prayers, collective identity, corporate image or elements of memory in relation to the Order of St John. However, this floor of floors is now equally important for our modern day visitors. The floor remains an object of study too, thanks to its religious, historical, cultural and touristic values. Although many slabs no longer mark the actual burial place of the deceased, the floor has retained its immense visual attractiveness. St John's is a 'living' church, as well as a museum. The floor is well looked after and the current programme of conservation of the St John's Co-Cathedral Foundation guarantees that St John's can maintain its round of daily religious services, while visitors may enjoy the spectacle of 'the most beautiful floor in the world.'

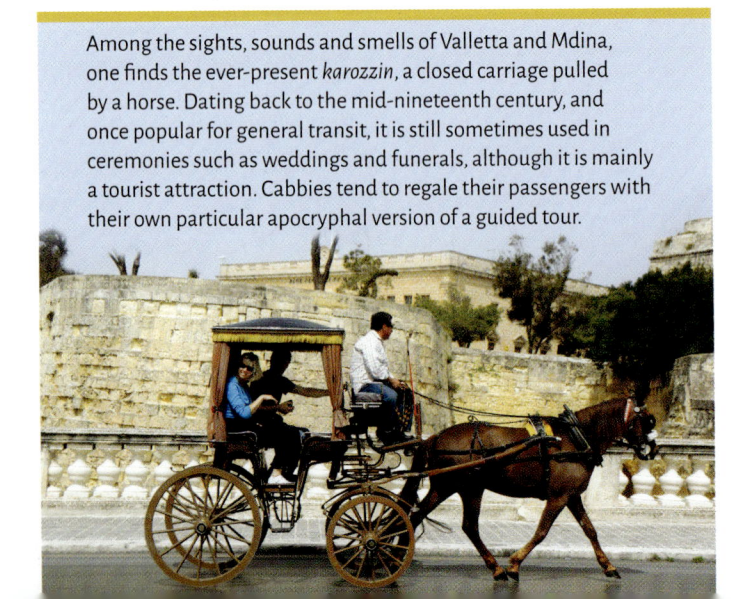

Among the sights, sounds and smells of Valletta and Mdina, one finds the ever-present *karozzin*, a closed carriage pulled by a horse. Dating back to the mid-nineteenth century, and once popular for general transit, it is still sometimes used in ceremonies such as weddings and funerals, although it is mainly a tourist attraction. Cabbies tend to regale their passengers with their own particular apocryphal version of a guided tour.

Hidden secrets of Valletta

VERONICA BARBARA

Upon entering Valletta through its modern gate, one is overwhelmed by the activity the city generates. Civil servants rushing along the main thoroughfares to reach their offices, people queuing in front of banks, shopkeepers opening their outlets, waiters laying out tables outside their restaurants, and the occasional pigeon looking for scraps... Among all this hustle and bustle it is very easy to miss a number of interesting details Valletta has to offer.

Some of the squares and streets of Valletta are so packed with shops of all kinds, artistic façades and imposing monuments that it is not surprising if visitors often notice only half of what there is to admire. Such is the case, for example, with St George's Square. Here your gaze immediately runs over the large entrances of the Grand Master's Palace, the Main Guard facing it, and the emotional monument of the Sette Giugno 1919 riots. You might not look up and observe the façade of the Grand Master's Palace enough to notice that the balconies at each corner are extremely long, and are decorated with exquisitely-carved stone supports. At the corner between Republic Street and Archbishop Street, beneath the palace balcony, there is a grotesque figure, similar to a gargoyle, commonly known in Maltese as the *'Beżża 'l-Art'* (scarer of the ground). It is a curious detail originally placed there in order to ward off the evil eye, and any evil spirits lurking in the shadows beneath.

Walking along Republic Street, just a few steps away from St George's Square, the visitor is once again surrounded by a number of things to observe. The

Valletta A PERSONAL CITY GUIDE

square adjacent to the Palace was initially called Piazza Tesoreria, since the treasury of the Knights of the Order of St John was situated here, precisely in the building which nowadays houses the social club Casino Maltese and the popular Caffe Cordina. On the façade of this building one can see a reproduction of a very complex sundial with zodiacal signs, the original unfortunately having been damaged during the bombings of World War II.

Dominating the square is a statue of Queen Victoria, reminiscent of the times when Malta formed part of the British Empire. In fact it was this statue that gave the name of 'Piazza Regina' to the space. When ties with the British were severed and Malta became a republic, the square was renamed Republic Square, a name which it still retains till this very day, although everybody still refers to in Maltese as '*Pjazza Reġina*'. The backdrop to the statue of Queen Victoria is one of the few buildings that were built by the Order of St John to serve a particular purpose, and are still used for that same purpose nowadays – the *Bibliotheca* or National Library. The façade is

A grotesque balcony bracket

a perfect example of a transitory period in art. It was built towards the end of the 18th century, when the baroque style was experiencing its decline and the new neoclassical trend was taking over. In fact, the architectural details of the National Library are a mix of both styles.

I am always surprised that although Valletta's museums and sites are pretty well-known, there are still some places which are hidden secrets, sometimes even for Maltese people living outside of Valletta. One such building is the University of Malta Valletta Campus. The Campus, originally built as a Jesuit college and residence in the late 16th century, has two entrances. The very first entrance was the one on Merchants Street. The other entrance, on St Paul Street, was added later on during the Colonial Period and is in the neoclassical style so favoured by the British. The inscription in Greek on top of the portico can be translated as 'knowledge is the gateway to success', a motto that fits perfectly with the building's purpose as a teaching institution. The Valletta Campus was the main campus of the University up to the mid-20th century, when the structure was deemed too small for the large number of courses offered and the steady increase in the student population, so a more extensive modern campus was constructed in nearby Msida.

Today, this beautiful building houses the University's Conferences and Events Unit, the International Collaborative Programmes Unit and the Research and Innovation Development Trust. Visitors can still admire the original pavement, the particular vaulted ceiling, along with a splendid library. A collection of casts, copies of original classical masterpieces, dates back from the time when the building served as a school of art. A recently refurbished black-box theatre is situated on the ground floor, and is extremely sought after by many theatrical companies on the Island. The renovation that the building is currently ongoing is aimed to enhance the precious architectural features of the building while introducing all the latest technological requirements needed for conferences and lectures.

Another site which is beautiful, but often neglected by many visitors, is Casa Rocca Piccola

Valletta A PERSONAL CITY GUIDE

in Republic Street, a city palace owned by the de Piro family, members of which still reside in the house till this very day. Each visit to the house offers a new discovery, as every room is packed with intriguing objects. My favourite piece of furniture in the house is a highly-ornate portable altar. When closed, it does not look any different from an armoire. When open, it contains all the necessary paraphernalia to celebrate Mass. The house is also furnished with a small chapel, which is not a surprising find in a domestic space in a noble home. In the past, noble families always had a small room or niche in the house reserved for holy prayer, and sometimes even religious ceremonies were held in private in this space.

Exploring the sumptuous spaces of Casa Rocca Piccola is a perfect taster of how a noble family lived in the 16th, 17th and 18th centuries. As you walk in the dining room, with the table laid out for dinner, and admire the numerous paintings hanging on the walls, you cannot help but feel transported back in time, to a world of luxury and artistic expression seldom encountered in modern times.

Casa Rocca Piccola

After experiencing such luxuries, I often cannot help but ponder about the people who made it all possible; the craftsmen who created the intricately-carved furniture, the skilled women who worked with fine textiles and, most of all, the builders who erected the impressive structures we still admire today. In Valletta, there is a centre dedicated to the work of a group of the working-classes to whom we owe the massive fortifications protecting the Maltese Islands. The 'Fortress Builders – Fortifications Interpretation Centre', situated at the end of St Mark Street, forms part of the Restoration Directorate of the Ministry of Justice, Culture and Local Government, and is co-financed by the European Regional Development Fund.

The entrance being free, and the staff extremely helpful and friendly, this interpretation centre is loved by all those who visit it, adults and children alike. Apart from extensive information on building techniques and interactive spaces ideal for children, the halls display detailed models of most of the fortifications of note, not just those protecting Valletta, Mdina

The Fortifications Interpretation Centre

and the Citadel in Gozo, but also the coastal watch-towers and countryside look-out posts. Taking the visitor chronologically from prehistoric times up to the British period, the Centre offers the perfect opportunity to fortification-enthusiasts to acquire the knowledge wanted before visiting the actual sites. I always feel that a visit to Fortress Builders is the perfect complement to a boat-ride within the Grand Harbour. I assure you that any visitors will be impressed by the massive walls and extensive defence systems of the harbour area and will appreciate them better, having previously learnt about the hard work and thorough planning involved in their construction.

After the visit to Fortress Builders, do not rush off to the centre of Valletta, but rather walk along Marsamxett Street, and take in the view of Marsamxett Harbour and the town of Sliema on the other side. Keep on walking until you reach a gun-post from the British era, which has been turned into a themed snack bar. Stop for a quick lunch, enjoying the pleasant breeze and the smell of the Mediterranean Sea just below.

At some point, you will decide to head back to the heart of the city and you will probably pop in to St John's Co-Cathedral, a must. It is one of the most sought-after attractions in Valletta. With its impressive interior, described by many art historians as the most beautiful church interior in Europe, one cannot leave out a visit to this building. A visit to St John's is a truly mesmerising experience. As soon as you step inside this sacred space, you are immediately overwhelmed by its golden walls, marbled floors and frescoed ceilings.

The beauty and richness of this church are so profuse that it is very easy to miss the smaller details, one of which is the chapel of Aragon, with its four funerary monuments of Grand Masters Nicolas Cotoner, Raphael Cotoner, Ramon Perellos y Roccaful and Martin de Redin. In reality a fifth Grand Master is also represented within the space – Grand Master Ramon Despuig. His image on the side of the altar is easily overlooked, along with his coat of arms on the other side. Despuig's image is eclipsed by the more elaborate baroque monuments of the brothers Cotoner. One of these monuments did not fit in completely within its intended spot and part of the wall had to be removed to make space for one of the angels' trumpet!

Standing in front of the presbytery, all kinds of works of art can be admired. Dominating the scene is the large main altar, decorated with *lapis lazuli*, and the titular sculpture of the Baptism of Christ carved in Carrara marble right behind it. Often, visitors spend so much time admiring this area, that they forget to turn around and observe the large lunette on top of the main doorway. The 'Allegory of the Triumph of the Order', along with the rest of the ceiling frescoes, is the work of the famous Italian master, Mattia Preti. Restored in recent years, as explained in detail by St John's Co-cathedral and Museum

Curator Cynthia de Giorgio (2013: 57-65), this beautiful work shows the three facets of the Order of St John - Hospitaller, Military and Naval. The two Grand Masters depicted are Nicolas and Raphael Cotoner, two brothers who succeeded each other in ruling the Order and who initiated the extensive project of decorating the interior of St John's. Nicolas is shown tending to the sick, whilst Raphael is pointing at a painting of the Order's galleys.

This Cathedral is renowned for the largest painting ever painted by the controversial Italian painter Caravaggio – *The Beheading of St John the Baptist*, a large canvas that can be admired in the Oratory. I remember seeing this painting for the first time when I was very young, perhaps seven years old, and I must admit it really impressed me. The scene being enacted by the characters is truly horrific but what impresses most is the realistic rendering of the figures, from the muscled executioner, to the old lady despairing for the martyr's fate with her hands covering her face. Many people spend up to half an hour staring at this masterpiece, taking in all its details, so much

Interior view of St John's Co-Cathedral

Valletta A PERSONAL CITY GUIDE

The Oratory of St John's with Caravaggio's only signed masterpiece

so that they forget to give enough attention to another painting by Caravaggio found in the same space. As they face the *Beheading*, this other work of art is situated behind them.

The painting of *St Jerome*, albeit much smaller in dimensions, is an equally impressive work, looking almost like a photograph in its realistic rendering. This Saint is believed to have lived in the desert where he translated the Bible, and so the talented artist portrayed his skin as being very pale except for his face and hands which are red and burnt, being the only parts of the body exposed to the sun. He is old and wrinkled, but with a determined expression, stylus in hand and the obligatory skull on his desk reminding all of mortality.

The sides of the Oratory also hold their own fascination. Symmetry being an essential component of the baroque style, Preti made sure to depict a series of fake windows on one side to balance the real windows on the other side. Some people say that no matter how many times they visit St John's Co-Cathedral, they still manage to discover something new every time. I must admit it happens to tourist guides as well!

Exiting from the Co-Cathedral and wandering along the busy streets, one is inevitably drawn in by one or two of the many shops spread all over the city. Local artisan work on sale includes glasswork, religious statuettes, intricate filigree jewellery and models, as well as miniatures carved in the local globigerina limestone. Sometimes you might be lucky enough to observe the actual craftsmen at work. You might even come across a few quirky shops such as Ċekċik, a small ethnic and vintage bazaar situated in Melita Street, very close to Castille Place.

To finish off the walk, a visit to the Upper Barrakka Garden is a must, especially because the magnificent view of the Grand Harbour from here is utterly

Valletta A PERSONAL CITY GUIDE

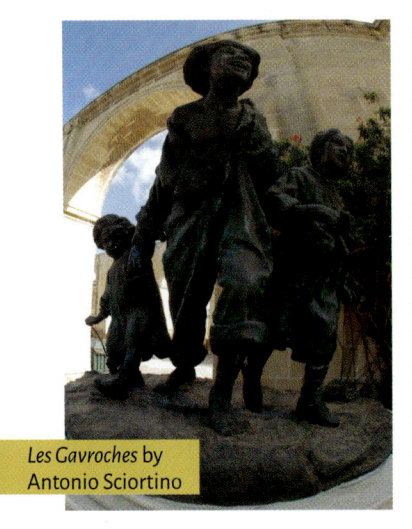

Les Gavroches by Antonio Sciortino

breathtaking. Keep in mind, however, that this garden is also a small outdoor museum of sculptures in its own right. The most famous monument is definitely the modern replica of '*Les Gavroches*'. Inspired by Victor Hugo's '*Les Miserables*', the talented Maltese sculptor Antonio Sciortino rendered, in a highly realistic manner, three poor children in tatters, wandering around the desolate streets of Paris during the French Revolution. This dynamic and exciting work, executed during Sciortino's early years, heavily contrasts the rather static monument of the Maltese politician Sir Gerald Strickland, done on commission without much feeling in the last years of the artist's life. Among the many other monuments spread around the garden, it is quite easy to miss a very simple one to British governor Sir Thomas Maitland. Nicknamed 'King Tom' and quite unloved by the local population, no grandeur was lavished on Maitland. Art critic Emanuel Fiorentino (2004: 29) describes it as a simple sarcophagus with a Latin cross lying on top. You really have to look for this monument in order to find it!

Valletta has so many hidden details that it would take a whole book to mention them all. Here I just wanted to draw the attention of visitors to those little things one usually misses upon a first visit. Of course, a first visit should serve as an aperitif to a second, a third and maybe even a fourth, thus ensuring enough time to discover the secret beauty and history of this unique cultural capital.

References:
De Giorgio, C. (2013) 'Mattia Preti's The Allegory of the Triumph of the Order', *Treasures of Malta* XIX:3 (57-65)
Fiorentino, E. (2004) 'Monuments at the Upper Barracca', *Treasures of Malta* XI:1 (25-32)

Our Caravaggio
NARCY CALAMATTA

There are sixty-five known Caravaggio paintings in the world. Two are in Malta. What is special about them is that they are native Maltese, and were not acquired from some other place, but were commissioned from, and painted by him specifically to hang where they are now. They were painted in 1608, the same year that Shakespeare wrote the great tragedy of King Lear, when Malta was ruled by the Order of the Knights Hospitallers of St John. These paintings were not recognised as masterpieces in their time, but they surely are now.

They were also ignored by Napoleon Bonaparte during his short pillaging visit to Malta in 1798, although there is a Caravaggio work of art, in the form of a contemporary portrait of Grand Master Wignacourt and his pageboy, at the Louvre today. Napoleon ousted the Knights and handed their Cathedral to the Maltese Catholic Church. In 1800, when the British arrived, assisting in the ousting of the French by the Maltese, they also stayed at arm's length, and so these two paintings have always remained in St John's Co-Cathedral.

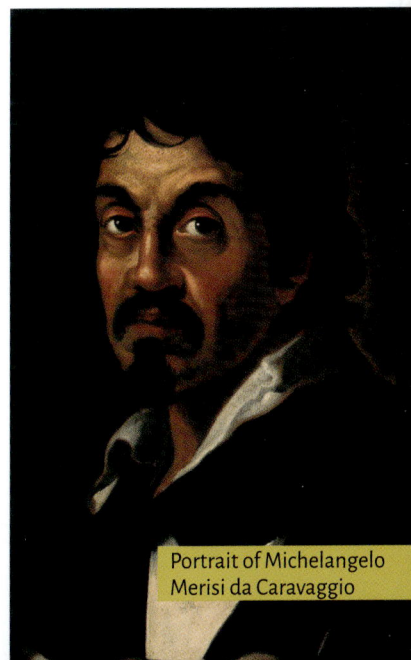

Portrait of Michelangelo Merisi da Caravaggio

Valletta **A PERSONAL CITY GUIDE**

Today every capital city in Europe craves a Caravaggio masterpiece. Valletta hosted the man for eighteen months. Born Michelangelo Merisi and raised in the city of Caravaggio, somewhere between Milano and Verona, he would eventually adopt Caravaggio as his pseudonym. He came to Malta by design when he was a fugitive after having committed murder in Rome.

He was orphaned at the age of 14 and trained as a painter in Milan. At the age of 20, he wanted to go down to Rome where the popes provided a lot of money for good artists. When his tutor was asked to recommend him, he wrote: "It takes a good master to make his student better than him."

Why did he write this? What had Michelangelo Merisi produced so far? Not much actually, but to his tutor's trained eye, Merisi's genius was apparent. At the time, over a century after Raffaello and Michelangelo, artists would do everything to try to make their mark on the art scene. They were painting in style which would become known as Mannerism. They would do anything to be different from the old masters, with one example being a Madonna holding a child

A contemporary painting of St John's Co-Cathedral

with such a long neck that it was apparently sired by a giraffe. In his early days in Rome, Merisi produced a still life of a basket of fruit. Other painters were in the habit of painting bowls of fruit with such beautiful fare that only in the excellence of heaven could such fruit exist. Merisi (Caravaggio), on the other hand, painted rotting fruit in a dirty, damaged basket framed by dark leaves, going brown with decay. He went even further, placing the basket just over the edge of a table, risking it falling off.

That is how he conducted his artistic, and indeed his real life from then on. Always walking on the edge of convention, he was an irritant to society. His first commissions in Rome were contested and removed immediately. He painted a tryptique of the life of St Matthew the Evangelist for the San Luigi dei Francesi church. This immediately landed him in trouble.

Convention respected saints as more important than living cardinals. A cardinal was considered a prince of the Church. Therefore, a saint had to look more glorious, richer and intangible. All Baroque Madonnas

The Oratory of the Beheading

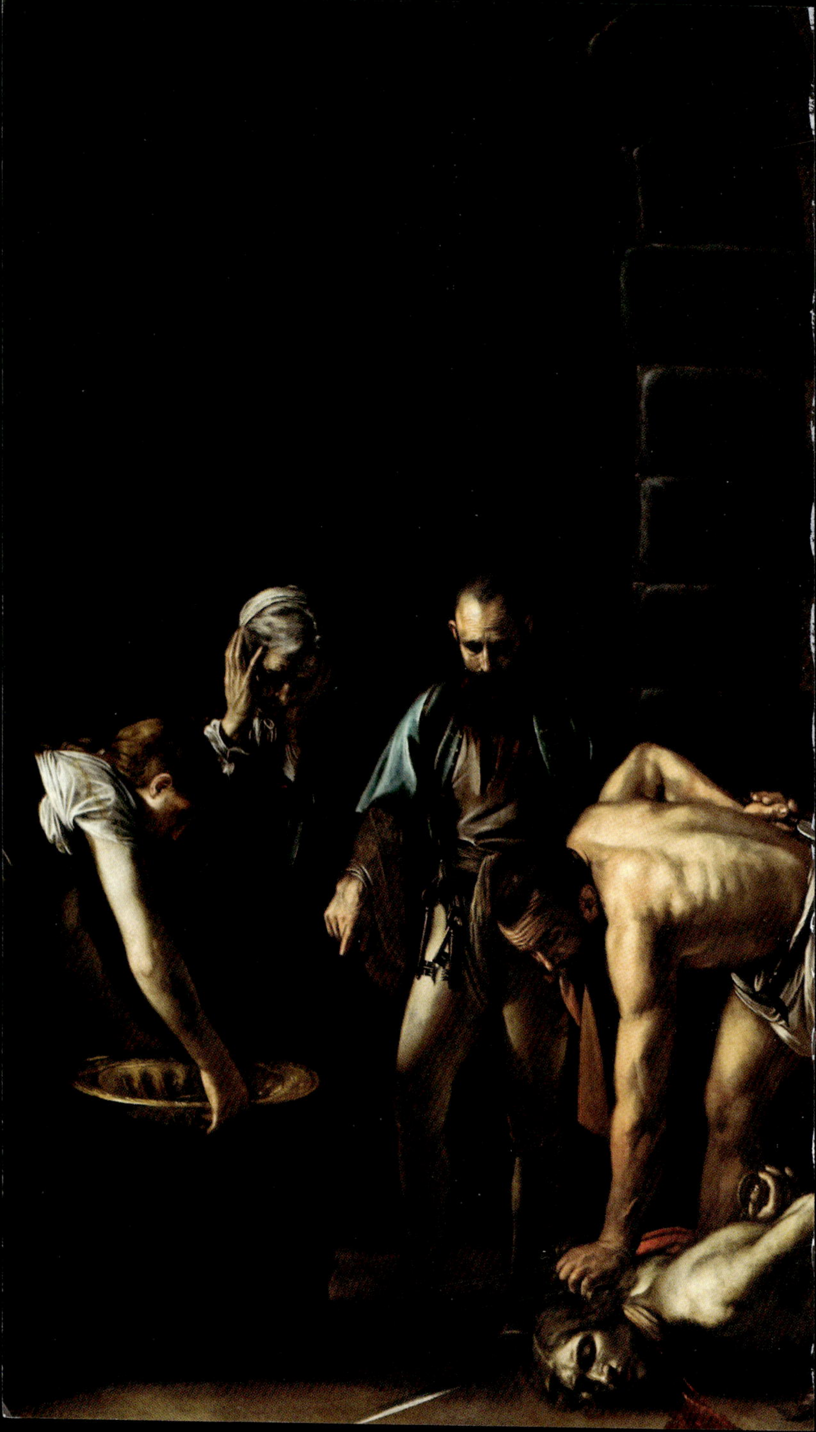

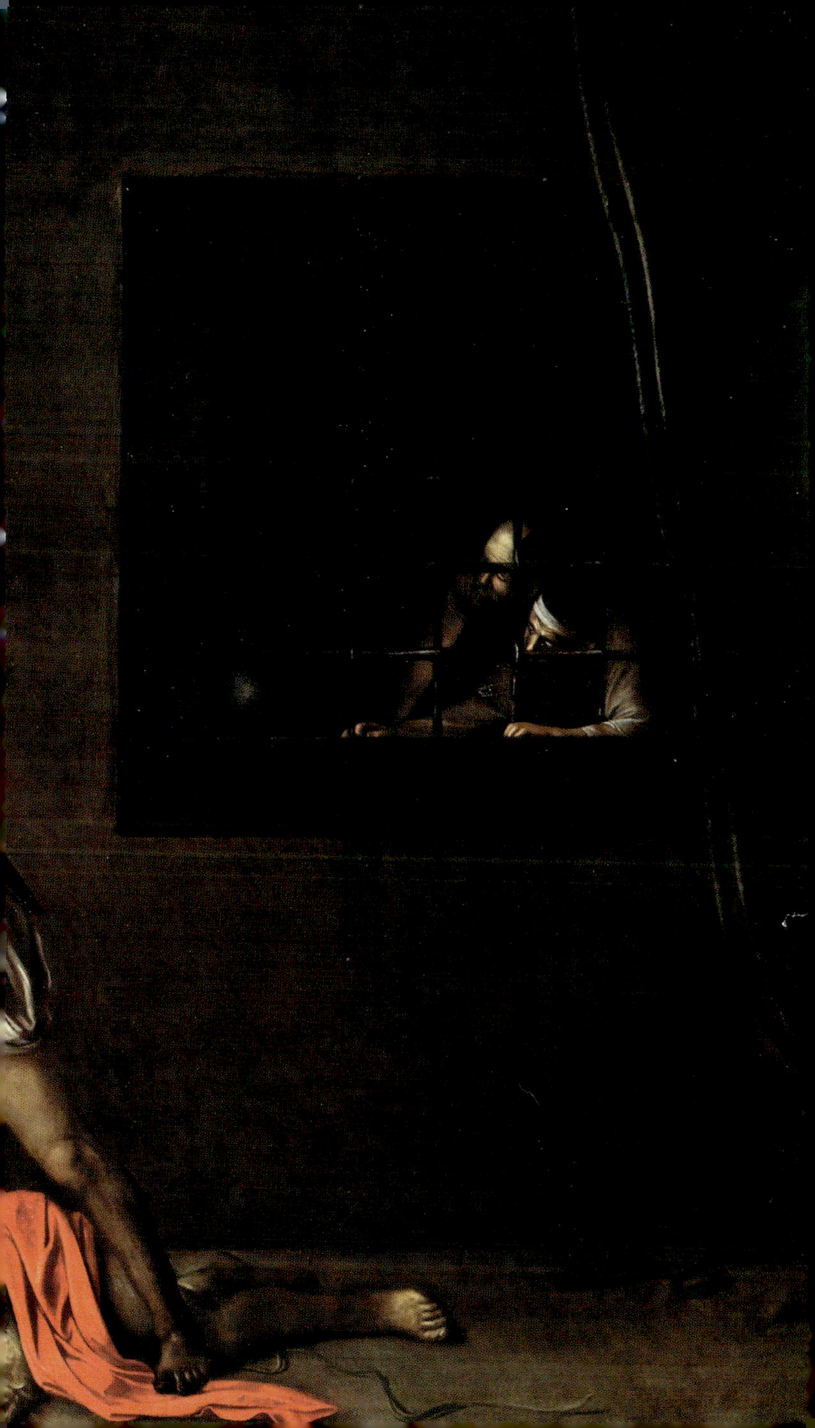

Valletta A PERSONAL CITY GUIDE

Caravaggio's signature

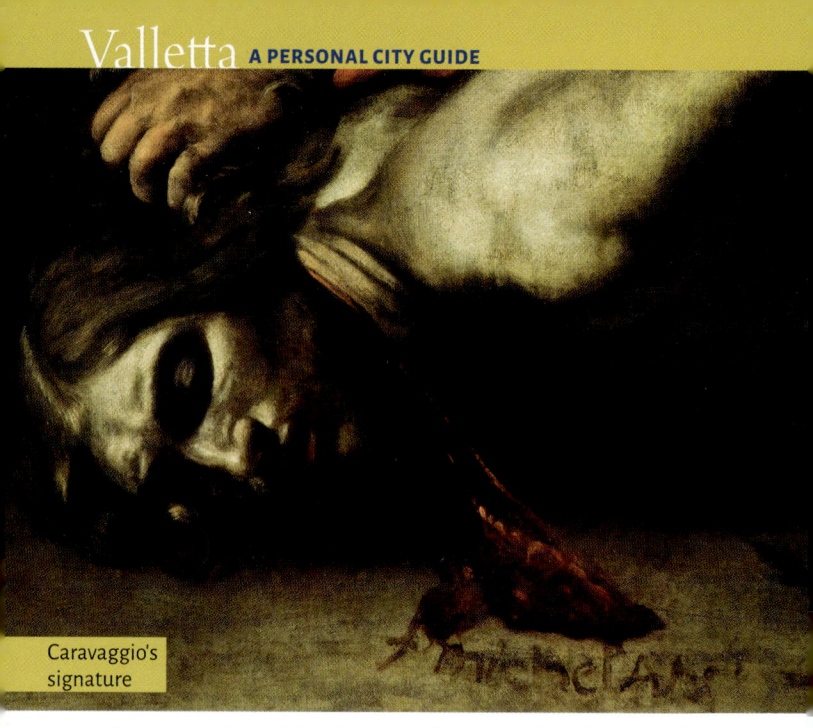

and saints are dressed in silk-and-gold-embroidered velvet or damask, and wearing gold sandals. They are always depicted being lifted up to heaven by a host of angels. This was the time of the Counter-Reformation, and it was a triumphant Church which was commissioning the artists. Their brief was clear - Depict saints in their '*Gloria*' and 'apotheosis', or rather going up to heaven to become one with God.

Our artist, the defiant Michelangelo Merisi, chose to paint St Matthew as a bald, old man in tatty rags, sitting on an enormous chair with his legs crossed, holding up a large book, and with his dirty bare feet presented to the viewer. The painting had been executed in such a way, that when the celebrating priest used to raise the consecrated bread, it would be exactly in line with the Saint's dirty foot. Out went the first St Matthew!

The side panel was then assured of a St Matthew wearing rich clothing, but as it was his martyrdom, he was shown lying on his back and battered by a handsome nude young man in the centre of the picture. What was worse was that St Matthew was drawn lying with his head nearer to the beholder, and therefore his feet pointing away towards the central vanishing point. Therefore the visual impression was that his feet were higher than his head. Nobody was going to pay good money for an upside-down saint! Out went the second St Matthew!

The Vatican rejected Merisi's first efforts, and replaced him with Guido Reni, an artist who knew what the church purchasers wanted. Merisi had few lay commissions and he became poor. No money made him hungry, and therefore an angry man. He was always quarrelling and was arrested at least four times till eventually, in a fight, he killed a man with strong political connections. He had to run away to Naples where he arranged with the family of a Knight of Malta to go to work for Grand Master Olaf de Wignacourt in Valletta. His new patron promised him a pardon from the Pope. Their relationship developed warmly and after a lot of study of the rules of the Order of St John, Michelangelo Merisi was installed and consecrated as a Knight of Malta only 12 months after he had arrived in Malta, where he adopted the name 'Caravaggio'.

Tradition demanded that a new knight should present his *'gioia'* (happiness) in a material expression of thanks. Caravaggio had nothing to offer so he promised a painting. He set out to paint the largest canvas ever stretched on a frame up till then with his choice of subject being, of course, the Patron Saint of the Order, St John the Baptist.

Three months later, the five metre by three metre masterpiece, *The Beheading of St John the Baptist* was ready and Caravaggio started preparing for the formal ceremony of presentation. He visited a brother knight who was the *'maestro di cappella'* or music master, of the Order and requested that the boys' choir would perform at the *'gioia'* presentation ceremony. The maestro di cappella refused unless he was well paid for his pains. Caravaggio had no money and the repeated refusal by the maestro to cooperate left him so frustrated and angry that he beat him up. Violence committed against a brother knight was, at the time, a crime punishable by death.

He was put in an underground prison of oblivion in Fort St Angelo at the tip of Vittoriosa. It is obvious that he was somehow helped, since he escaped just three days later in order to avoid execution. He soon re-appeared painting in Sicily where, once again, he got in trouble with an important family who chased him all the way to Naples. There they beat him up badly, and the few friends he had left put him on a boat and dropped him at Porto Ercole, a few miles outside Rome. Eventually, he was found dead in the street. Ironically enough, just a day later, the pardon for his first crime, the murder in Rome, was issued by the Pope.

Michelangelo Merisi di Caravaggio started his public painting life at the age of 20, and died at the age of 39. He was not well understood so he got few commissions. He never signed any of his paintings, not even those that were not sacred. So over the years few new finds have cropped up to add to his oeuvre. That is why Malta is somewhat unique to have these two works of art – *The Beheading of St John the Baptist* and the *St Jerome* …

After World War II, the *Beheading* was kept behind closed doors and the smaller one, *St Jerome* was hung high on the sidewalk of the Italian langue chapel. Michelangelo Merisi da Caravaggio had not as yet been really recognised. It was only in the 60s, when the Italian art historian specialised in Italian Renaissance painting, Federico Zeri, wrote a treatise encouraging art lovers to have another look at his works that the whole Caravaggio oeuvre lit up.

Zeri had insisted that since this painter was so controversial in his time, then his works' appreciation should be made from a personal point of view. Praise flowed in from all over the world. Caravaggio was hailed as the first of the Moderns, notwithstanding that he painted four hundred years ago. He became known as the master of realism and symbolism. The fact that he painted his saints upside-down made him even more endearing.

When at the age of 49, I decided to retire from my filmmaking career and read for a degree in Theatre Studies and Communications, I was introduced to the great Caravaggio by my old friend the Dominican Friar Fr Marius Zerafa, who was then the Curator of our National Museum of Fine Arts.

He was the national promoter of our Caravaggio paintings and imbued me with a sense of great respect and admiration for Caravaggio's works. Whereas most Maltese usually see our Caravaggio paintings maybe once or twice in a lifetime, my new career as a tourist-guide has me visiting them at least once a week. Although an admirer, I still felt frustrated, as I always felt that I was missing something, till I decided to follow Zeri's advice and look at our Caravaggio through my own eyes. For me *The Beheading of St John* is a work tantamount to a still from a post-war, Italian neo-realistic film. We see a naked man being squashed on the ground having his throat slit as one would kill a goat. Today we all know the feeling of such gruesome scenes with terrorists using web-streamed beheadings as the most cruelly effective means of generating global fear. This beheading scene is now not alien to us. It is not an artistic expression, but an act of defamation against human life. Whoever painted this canvas had something important to say.

The *Beheading* is not some triumphant 'apotheoses'. We do not see a saint richly dressed with gold sandals levitating towards heaven, accompanied by two cherubims on the left and two on the right, all riding on fluffy white clouds. There is no reference to Christian ritual here. It is rather pagan symbolism that tells the story realistically. The victim has a scarlet cloth draped over him. The Classics used to reserve the use of scarlet only for gods or kings. Therefore, the artist is telling us that notwithstanding the stark and naked reality of the shocking scene depicted, the victim was a man of import.

In the Renaissance (when this painting was painted), when a noble man was executed he was not seen suffering in public, and the executioner would use a long and heavy sword to make sure he died with one stroke. Here we see the long sword lying by the victim. It had not done the trick and the executioner is reaching for the short knife of mercy to finish the job. The condemned man is not yet dead.

Caravaggio had studied this subject thoroughly. He was a fugitive and there was a price on his head. He painted beheadings repeatedly. He painted the severed head of Medusa from Greek mythology and he also left a painting of an episode in the Bible showing Judith beheading the enemy's leader, Holifernes, after

157

getting him drunk. There are two versions of David and Goliath, with the last one being an appeal for clemency from the Pope by putting his own face as Goliath, while writing to the Pope to see to what misery he had been reduced. In all four pictures mentioned here, the face of the victim is that of a desperate person.

It is not so in our *Beheading*. Here St John the Baptist is still serene, knowing that it will not be long before he will meet his God in heaven. The man is also shown wearing a lamb's skin when in the Gospel it is written that he wore camel skin. Here Caravaggio is using his artistic licence to show St John as a sacrificial lamb.

Then we come to the enigma of the crowd of people standing around. Already we see the controversy that everyone is restricted to half of the canvas and pushed away in a corner. Women attending such a heinous crime are not conventional. You could say it is a realistic composition but there must be more to it than that.

Let us take them one at a time, when this painting was made in 1608, Caravaggio had just been installed as a Knight of St John. To become a Knight he had to take the vows of poverty, chastity, obedience and charity. This was still fresh in his mind. It was his new conviction.

Perhaps the maid carrying a large solid gold dish is to remind him that he must say no to gold. The Greek tragedy character of the wailing old woman could depict the fact that a knight must refuse to have his own family, and cut links even with his mother. The steward pointing at the action with a finger backed by heavy keys of responsibility must be reminding Caravaggio that he must now submit to being obedient to authority. Finally, there is the cold cruelty of the executioner counter-pointing the creed of the Knights whose guiding light is love (charity) not violence. There we see that symbolism is underpinning the realism of the socio-political circumstance of the painting, linking history with current artistic execution. The purpose of this painting was to make the viewer meditate and reach out for the catharsis that it offers.

Caravaggio must have felt he was creating a masterpiece, his artistic opus. This is the only painting he ever signed. At the point of the painting where the blood is shown oozing from the neck and flowing

St Jerome

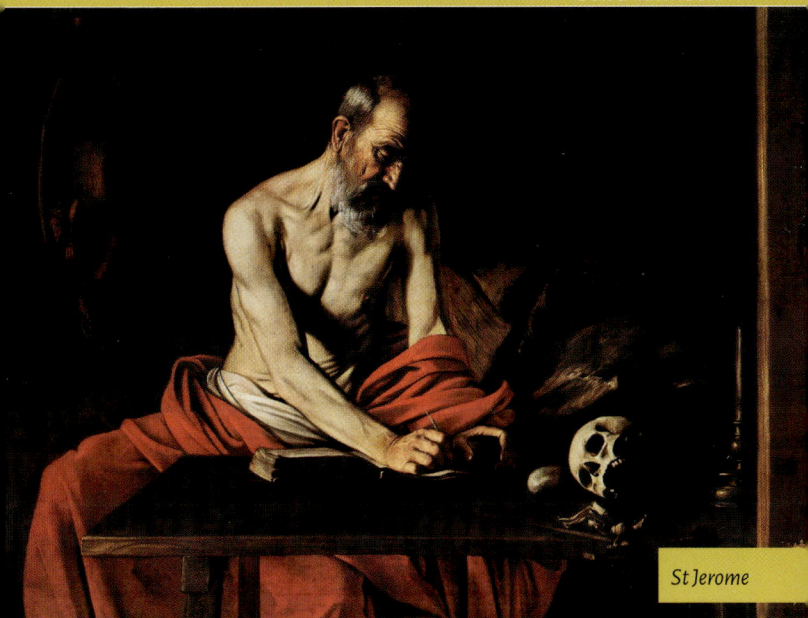

on to the ground, Caravaggio wrote in the same colour as the blood, the letter 'F' followed by his name, Michelangelo – Frà Michelangelo.

While the *Beheading* is undoubtedly Caravaggio's greatest work, facing it there is the smaller portrait of St Jerome. This was Caravaggio's third attempt at this subject. St Jerome was the hermit who translated the Gospels from classical Greek to the 'vulgar' Latin. The Pope had offered to make him a Cardinal, a prince of the Church, but Jerome refused, wanting to live in the desert like St John the Baptist.

You must see for yourselves the realism and the symbolism. The rejected cardinal's hat is seen hanging in the dark on the wall. Observe the emaciated, naked, old man with battle scars on his face. Some say that the face is that of Grand Master Wignacourt. Then take in the rest, starting with the scarlet red cloak, the pebble for self flagellation and the skull depicting mortality. There is also death shown in the candle without the life of a flame. What is the old man writing? Maybe the episode when Jesus tells Nicodemus that he must die in spirit before he is born again to the new life. Jesus did not just talk the talk, but also walked the walk. He accepted suffering the most vilifying death for any Jew under the occupying forces of the Romans, and that is death by crucifixion. The victim was not killed and hanged, but stripped naked and left to die hanging on a cross. The cruellest death of all, when one is left to die slowly, and to choke on his own blood.

Caravaggio first painted this St Jerome scene with the Saint writing with one hand, and holding a crucifix in the other. Another version has the crucifix standing on a candlestick. The one in the Oratory of St John's Co-Cathedral in Malta has the crucifix pushed to one corner in the dark. It is almost falling off the table. It is abandoned as the ultimate shameful end to life. Caravaggio might have been saying that to be born again in sanctity, you have to let your worldly and materialistic self go completely. What is hard to swallow in this case is that the crucifix has the head pointing at the viewer and the feet slightly higher pointing at the vanishing point. Jesus is depicted in the characteristic Caravaggio presentation of being upside-down. That is blasphemous from any point of view.

However, Caravaggio must have wanted us to feel this indignity and rise to defend our faith. He was undoubtedly very controversial for his time, and his life evidences this to the max.

St Jerome is a famous painting in the art world. On New Year's Eve in 1984, it was stolen, having been cut out of the frame. It was then taken abroad to be sold to underworld collectors. No one took the risk of buying it to avoid being traced by Interpol. The thief brought it back to Malta, and sent a sliver of the canvas to my friend Fr Zerafa, asking for ransom money to return the painting. Fr Zerafa went along and promised him the money, involving the police in the operation. After two years, eight months from the robbery and on the 4 August 1987, the police and Fr Marius Zerafa retrieved the *St Jerome* and arrested the gang members. It emerged that the gang had paid £5,000 to have Fr Marius kidnapped during the exchange. Our *St Jerome* is now occupying pride of place in the Oratory, facing the much larger *Beheading*, but sharing equally in its glory and in the admiration they both enjoy from the thousands of visitors who are left enthralled by the sheer dynamism of the art packed into one single room.

Musical Band Clubs and the Village Feast

PAUL SPITERI

Symphonic Band Clubs in Malta are the pride of our towns and villages and play a strong role in Maltese social culture. Their majestic palatial houses situated in the village core are a social meeting place for locals who gossip, play snooker or pool, have a drink, or a simple snack. These clubs also organise activities connected with the local village festa the Maltese name for the village feasts celebrating patron saints of towns, and villages.

The activities of the band club include the preparation of street decorations for these feasts, or managing the fireworks production used for these occasions. Band clubs in Malta are part and parcel of the social and cultural history of the Maltese Islands and have, over the years, established themselves as an institution in the core of every town and village, aimed at spreading Maltese culture and the teaching of music. Many musicians who have gone on to make a name for themselves, domestically or abroad, owe their success, in part, to the encouragement and teaching of the local band club.

The premises of most of these clubs are attractions in themselves, places to show off musical memorabilia as well as souvenirs of major achievements over the years. They offer a meeting place for members and a teaching place where young musicians are encouraged to join their colleagues in the next village festivities. Musical programmes along the main streets of the village herald a week of festivities and celebrations. Feasts are mainly held between June and September and usually, more than one is celebrated every weekend.

If you have flown in to visit Valletta, the European Capital of Culture 2018, make it a point to go to one of the village feasts held in several towns and villages surrounding the Valletta harbour, mingle with the locals and enjoy the merrymaking provided by the band marches. Don't forget to taste the traditional Maltese delicacies offered at one of the many street food outlets, set up for this special occasion! You could as well take a village stroll through the labyrinth of winding narrow streets, and enter the village band club premises, especially in the evenings, for a refreshing pint of beer or a cup of tea or coffee and a snack.

Band clubs as we know them today started in the second half of the 19th-century, when Malta was ruled by the British and there was an influx of Italian refugees escaping from the civil war raging in Italy. At this point, wind instruments had become popular. Malta was thriving as a British base and musical repertoires played by the clubs were excerpts of popular operas played at the Valletta Royal Opera Theatre built in 1861. Small bands were being formed. In some parishes, there were not enough persons who could afford to buy instruments, so the community, with the help of some merchants, intervened to help those who were ready to learn. The first band clubs were formed, and their main purpose was to take part in the village *festa*.

Every town and village in Malta and Gozo has its own band club, some even have two, as there are certain villages which celebrate two feasts – one dedicated to the patron saint and the other celebrating the so-called 'secondary' feast of another saint. In the past, unfortunately, an intense rivalry developed when a village had more than one club, and this rivalry at times became violent as each struggled to better the other when it came to the celebration of 'their' Saint.

In Valletta, in particular, a dichotomy was established between persons wanting to play the sacred music by the anglophone Vincenzo Bugeja (1806-60), and his rival italianate Paolo Nani (1814-1904). The band club which favoured Bugeja bore the symbol of the star whilst the symbol of Nani was the eagle. Up to WWII, Italian was spoken by the Bourgeoise, the Judiciary, the Church and the University, while many other Maltese served in the British Navy and Military. In our capital city, Valletta, the 'La

MALTA BAND CLUBS AND THE VILLAGE FEAST

Valletta **A PERSONAL CITY GUIDE**

The statue of St Paul returning in the church after the procession

Vallette Band Club' was sponsored by confraternities appertaining to the Parish of St Paul and supported by persons belonging to the Nationalist Party – 'Partito Nazionalista'. On the other hand, the 'King's Own Band Club' was supported by the British. From 1874 till today it participates in the feast day of Saint Dominic, whose feast is also celebrated in Valletta. The 'King's Own Band Club' served as an important social, political and musical club for many people. It has always attracted attention from foreign visitors to the islands. When His Royal Highness Prince Philip, the Duke of Edinburgh, visited the club's premises on 28 November 1952, he stated: "I hope that this, my visit to the King's Own Band Club, will be interpreted as if I had been to all the band clubs of Malta."

After first turbulent, and then conciliatory circumstances, the Band Clubs Association was formed in 1947. The Association has just celebrated its 60th anniversary, endorsing a membership of 84 band clubs from all over the islands. According to the latest survey by the local National Statistics Office, the total number of bandsmen/women (*bandisti*) amounts to over four thousand, both residents and trainees, more than a quarter of whom are women.

Nowadays, however, this competitiveness is used in a more positive way, with rival band clubs leaving no stone unturned as they strive to decorate the façade of the club's premises in the most colourful and vivid way, to launch new musical numbers, and to create the most merry-making atmosphere possible. Marching in rows of six, wearing uniforms, and proudly showing off the badge of their club, a band is normally composed of between 60 and 70 bandsmen/women playing a variety of instruments.

In the 69 towns and villages in Malta and Gozo, there are more than 140 village feasts organised in any one year. The *festa,* as it is known in Maltese, is a week-long activity. Musicians participate in the external religious processions. The entire village comes to a festive life where the streets and squares are festooned with colourful flags, banners, statues of saints, angels and biblical prophets. These statues line the village square. The façade of churches and palaces are all colourfully lit up. The interior of the church is enriched by red damask. Flowers and highly-

Valletta **A PERSONAL CITY GUIDE**

Festas are time for celebration

decorated solid silver or gilded candlesticks adorn the altars. Crystal chandeliers hang from the ceilings, adding sparkle to the finery adorning the interior. At the Grand Finale of the feast there are aerial firework displays showing off the latest pyrotechnic mastery.

In conclusion, visitors are welcome to go to Valletta and the rural villages, to the parish square, and observe the louvred façades of these band clubs. The internet sites *www.maltaband.org* and *www.thechurchinmalta.org* give information about all the band clubs in Malta and Gozo, and also have an on-line calendar for all the *festas*. If small groups are organised, tourist guides will be only too willing to accompany them to these occasions, with reservations being made through the Malta Union of Tourist Guides *mutgsecretary@gmail.com* or *www.visitmalta.com*. Alternatively, there are several excursion organisers who have their reps at the major hotels who can advise you of *festa* events for larger groups, which take individual bookings, throughout 2018. Moreover, you can visit a local bookshop or websites stocking well-documented books such as *The Maltese Village Festa – A Traditional Yearly ritual* edited by Godfrey Farrugia or *The Village Feast – The Cultural Legacy of Malta & Gozo* by Vincent Zammit, *Maltese Feasts and Factions – Festa Partiti* by Jeremy Bossevain, and *Il-Knejjes Parrokkjali ta' Malta u l-Festi Taghhom* by Michael Schiavone.

The tourist guide will certainly feed you with humorous anecdotes, village gossip, vibes, and folklore tales to add sparkle to your festive village mood!

Cinematic Cityscape
NARCY CALAMATTA

What is one thing that Brad Pitt and Stephen Spielberg have in common? They both fell in love with Valletta as a versatile film set. They have both filmed in it, creating myriad locations, but never using Valletta as itself.

Brad Pitt was here in Malta three times, once to shoot 'Troy' (2003), a Greek Mythology epic, then to shoot 'World War Z' (2013), a dystopian futuristic block-buster, and three years ago he was here with his then wife, Angelina Jolie, to shoot a love story based in the South of France, 'By the Sea' (2014).

Spielberg shot 'Munich' (2004) here and he used Malta to portray various cities in Europe and Israel. He was here for so long that he became part of the scenery. He used to visit restaurants, shops and places of interest in Valletta without any fuss. The locals respected the gentleman for his work and never bothered him or

Justin Kurzel's *Assassin's Creed*, 2012

Valletta A PERSONAL CITY GUIDE

his family in their moments of rest.

One day, someone called out to Brad Pitt when he was scouting for locations in one of the steep streets of Valletta. A crowd of shoppers shouted out his name repeatedly. He was not pleased and kept on going with his work. However, he sent an assistant to apologise to the callers. They were tourists from the UK over-excited at seeing a Hollywood-star, just a few metres away from them.

Burbank Syndrome

The Maltese today have what I call the Burbank Syndrome. They are all film-makers, or are related to, or know someone who works in the world of films. Many pensioners are film extras. Younger ones are film tradesmen, while others are cinema students or wannabe actors and script-writers.

The name for this syndrome comes from when Hollywood city spilled into nearby Burbank. Every waiter or taxi-driver there all of a sudden became involved in the film industry. Such people do not get over-excited when they see a film-star, because they would have seen her/him at work sweating it out for several days.

For us, these famous people are colleagues. We love them with a certain camaraderie that comes with frequent contact. That is why I describe this self-confident air about us as the Burbank Syndrome.

Ridley Scott's *Gladiator*, 2000

CINEMATIC CITYSCAPE

Olly's last one 'for the road'

In Valletta, restaurant waiters and taxi-drivers all have a special anecdote to tell over and over again of their favourite personality from the film industry, who was their client. The darling of British film-fans, Oliver Reed, was having a Sunday morning drink in a bar simply called The Pub. He was having a break from filming the Roman epic, 'Gladiator' (1999), with Russell Crowe in the main role. All of a sudden, the pub-owner noticed that Olly was lying on one of the long benches in the pub, motionless. That was his last drink for the road, the long road.

Now The Pub has become a shrine to Olly's memory and most British tourists have made it their must-visit Valletta landmark. The Maltese are very proud of this anecdote about the unique Oliver Reed, who filmed in Malta five times.

Visual historical name-dropping

This Maltese affinity with famous personalities is part of the history of Valletta. Ever since British Admiral Lord Horatio Nelson kicked out the Napoleonic troops from Malta, other famous names walked the streets of Valletta as if it were their home.

The Pub the real location of Oliver Reed's demise

The poet Lord Byron stopped over frequently on his way to and from the Levant. He had a problem with one of his legs and he hated climbing the steep steps of the undulant streets. Can you imagine him in the summer heat walking up St Ursula Street, the one with the San Francisco effect? In one of his poems he called "Valletta, The cursed city of steps".

Another Victorian poet, Lord Tennyson, stigmatised Valletta by calling it "The city of yells, bells and smells". These are visual impressions that became known world-wide, but perhaps the most appropriate remains Sir Walter Scott's description of Valletta as the "city built by gentlemen for gentlemen".

169

Valletta **A PERSONAL CITY GUIDE**

Directors of photography galore

Film-makers are the poets of today. They replicate the existential experience of Valletta on screen. The one who really makes the images is the Director of Photography (DOP). He is the one who manipulates the light and gives the image depths and levels to make a deep impression on the viewer.

Steven Spielberg's *Munich*, 2005

Most DOPs who come to work in Malta on major movies are Oscar-winners. I had the good fortune to work with quite a few, mostly as one of the director's assistants. The first one I met and worked with was in 1968 on the film 'Hieronymus Merkin', the lighting guru, Otto Heller. Eventually, there would also be Ossy Morris who in 1972 worked with John Huston on 'The MacKintosh Man', and Ted Moore who worked in 1978 on the TV series 'Martian Chronicles', starring Rock Hudson. These and other Anglo-Saxon cinematic historical figures made Valletta their atelier.

From Italy, I had the privilege to work with two of Federico Fellini's favourite DOPs - with

Tonino Delicolli, on Disney's 'Trenchcoat', where I had played the part of a tourist guide (25 years before I actually became a real tourist guide), and with Peppino Rotunno on the Robert Altman film 'Popeye the Sailor Man' (1980) with Robin Williams (in his first major role) as Popeye himself. With the help of some 30 Italian specialists and 100 Maltese tradesmen, we had built a film-set in Mellieha specifically for this film. I was the studio boss then, and decided to assume the responsibility of calling it Popeye Village and opening it as a tourist attraction. It still stands today.

Jump out of the screen

DOPs all have one thing in common, their intuitive sense of light management. Those of us who have lived in Valletta know where to walk according to the time of day and the season. The builders of Valletta wanted a planned city with all streets stretched in two sets of parallel straight lines, at right-angles to each other. Therefore, the sun, travelling from East to West, always casts a shadow on a choice number of streets, and we residents know where we can walk in the shade at any given time.

For a cinematographer, this is a wonderful co-operation by nature. That is why they film the stepped streets at a certain time, when the edges of the steps are high-lighted by the sun, making them jump out of the screen.

Alan Parker's *Midnight Express*, 1978

Valletta **A PERSONAL CITY GUIDE**

DOPs are aided by production designers, who change an environment to any demand made by the script. On the film '13 Hours' (2016), they dressed up East Street, the one where there is a bridge leading to a winding open staircase to Victoria Gate, as an authentic ethnic market in Libya. It was so realistic that when I first drove through it, I could not remember what it had looked like before.

Upstairs downstairs ride

In 1969 I worked on 'Eyewitness'. The young director, Johnny Hough, used St Ursula Street where it meets St John's Street at right angles, for a chase scene. Imagine two police motorcycles coming down the steps of St John's Street and climbing all the way up the steps of St Ursula Street to Barracca Gardens. We also had a Lamborghini drive down St Ursula Street.

The star scene was when the driver of a Mercedes coupé, supposedly carrying an African dignitary, is shot and the car bounces out of control, down the steps of Archbishop Street on the side of the Auberge D'Aragon. All of the people of Valletta had come out for the shooting of that scene. All the offices and shops lost most of their staff for two hours, when they went to see the stuntman pretend he had been shot, and yet at the same time, driving the Mercedes smoothly down the steps and crashing it into the corner. It went so well that the producer paid extra to make the stuntman do it a second time to a deafening, spontaneous applause from thousands of lookers-on.

Baroque background to foreground

Fifty years ago the Maltese were not yet the film aficionados they are today. 'Assassin's Creed' (2016) opened a new chapter in film-making in Valletta. The Baroque architecture of the churches and palaces were no longer the embellishing background but they actually became the action foreground.

Johnny Hough's *Eyewitness*, 1970

CINEMATIC CITYSCAPE

Kenneth Branagh's *Murder on the Orient Express*, 2017

Maltese professional stuntmen, with their foreign colleagues, have immortalised the rooftops of Valletta in a cutting edge, life-threatening set of choreographed fights that leave you breathless. The scenes are so realistic and they left such an impact on me that, every time I pass under the covered bridge linking the Grand Master's Palace to the Bibliotheca, I cross my fingers, glance up and hasten my pace, in case one of those swordsmen jumps down like a lightning-bolt and rips the buttons off my jacket.

Fingers Crossed

Every time I cross from Merchant's Street to Queen's Square and pass under the covered bridge linking the Frankly once I get there I would rather sit under an umbrella outside Caffe Cordina's and sip a fresh orange juice, hoping Ms Angelina Jolie will come along and sit with me to discuss her next artistic drama script to be filmed in Valletta's cinematic landscape.

As recently as 2017, Valletta once again lent itself to the silverscreen. Kenneth Branagh directed the film version of Agatha Christie's *Murder on the Orient Express* in which he also played the lead role as Hercule Poirot. The first few minutes see Valletta transformed magically as Jerusalem and the Grand Harbour doubling as a middle eastern port. It is indeed a timeless city with an international character – a most ideal film set.

173

Valletta A PERSONAL CITY GUIDE

VICTORIA GATE

Stories of a tourist guide
Viva viva l-Karnival!
VERONICA BARBARA

A new tourist guide's worst nightmare? Accepting a booking months in advance, only to realise closer to the date that it is a tour of Valletta during Carnival weekend! This is what happened to me a few years ago at the very start of my guiding career. I was worried about so many things... how was I expected to keep the group together? It was only a group of twenty persons, but streets in Valletta during Carnival are packed with people, all of them pushing and jostling each other to move from one area to another. And how was I expected to explain about the historic details when all one will be able to hear is the loud party music from the celebrations? How was I to point to the architectural features with floats and decorations blocking the view? What if the members of the group are not aware that it was going to be Carnival weekend and they actually hate noise and confusion?

There was nothing that I could do as such, except to ask the agency involved to let the group know what they were to expect… and wait for the day to arrive with a degree of trepidation.

On the day, I showed up at *Putirjal* (a local corruption of 'Porta Reale', the main entrance to Valletta) all flustered and trying to spot a group of people looking for me among the costume-wearing crowds eager to join the revelry in the city. I was holding a sheet of A4 paper with the name of the group typed on it, hopefully making me easy to identify. People did not stop staring at me, trying to understand whether I was impersonating someone or not. It was an extremely cold and windy February, and there was a dark heavy cloud hovering above.

Finally the group arrived. The ages were mixed, and I noticed a few grumpy elderly ladies too. One of them finally spotted me and signalled to the others to gather around me. I introduced myself but realised they couldn't really hear me properly so I raised my voice slightly. After my introduction about Valletta, I explained briefly what Carnival means to the Maltese, especially to the residents of Valletta, many of whom spend months preparing for this special event. I tried to prepare them for what they were about to experience. They smiled patronisingly in return. They probably thought that I was exaggerating.

We dived into the chaos, with me trying to explain about the Royal Opera House and why it is in ruins, but my clients could not even see the ruins as all its steps and stones were covered by people, sitting down, standing or jumping. Someone bumped into me while I was halfway through the story of the construction problems of the theatre, and a young member of the group giggled uncontrollably. Turning my head, I immediately saw why. I had just been almost knocked over by a human-sized banana!

We moved on, and I was struggling to stick to my usual historic and artistic commentary when a group of dancers dressed in colourful feathery costumes split my group in half and I realised that none of my clients were paying any attention at all to what I was saying. How could they when, right in front of them, there was a huge float, the most splendid I have ever seen, with mechanised figures on all sides and a highly elaborate rendering of a lion in the centre. I finally woke up to the fact that my group did not really care about the cold stone buildings and the static closed balconies, no matter how beautiful they are. It is the vibe of Valletta and its people which they craved, the excitement Carnival brings, the brightness of colours and the awesome talent of the men and women who bring cloth and papier-mâché to life with their imaginative creations. And I also understand that the noise, which had been my biggest worry, was one of the most attractive characteristics of this feast, an aspect which made my clients unwind, relax and let go of their inhibitions. Even the grumpy elderly ladies were laughing and clapping as a middle-aged man

VIVA VIVA L-KARNIVAL!

from the group started to dance and jump around with a group of pirates. This is Carnival. This is Valletta.

A Christian feast preceding Lent and its restrictions, it is generally accepted that Carnival in Malta dates back to at least the fifteenth century. Noise was always a very important component since, as Anna Borg Cardona explains (2014: 46), Carnival was also linked to pre-Christian rituals which marked the end of winter and the approaching of spring, a period when demons were believed to roam the earth. Noise was the antidote to keep them away. Nowadays, loud music and improvised instruments are not used to protect from evil spirits but rather to raise spirits! Music and a handful of *perlini* (sugar-coated almonds), and perhaps also a piece of *prinjolata* (a typical Maltese Carnival sweet) is the best combination for four days of revelry and entertainment. A few forgotten traditions are now also being reintroduced such as the *qarċilla*, a vulgar but extremely entertaining people's performance.

By the end of the day, returning home exhausted but rather satisfied with my experience, I knew that I had been silly to be afraid of guiding in Valletta during Carnival. Yes, I might not have given my group the amount of historic content I am used to giving and they will probably not tell their relatives and friends back home how intricately carved the façades are, or how many monuments there are in the streets of the city. But, closing my eyes, I can imagine those elderly ladies sitting next to their grandchildren and gesticulating with their hands while they narrate how joyous and colourful and bustling with energy the vibe in the Maltese capital during their visit had been.

References
Borg Cardona, A. (2014) Carnival and the power of sound, Treasure of Malta, XX 2: 45-49

Valletta and its harbours

PAUL SPITERI

Being a peninsula, Valletta is flanked by two bodies of water, both natural harbours. Through the ages the socio-economic development of the City has taken place hand-in-hand with the economic activity of these two harbours - Marsamxett Harbour on Valletta's north-west flank, and Grand Harbour on its south-east.

Napoleon is quoted as having once said, "The geography of a place shapes its history". These two safe harbours, in the heart of the Mediterranean, have attracted dominant powers and civilisations of the time since the first settlers came to the Maltese Islands over seven thousand years ago. Being right in the middle of what was then the sea occupying the centre of the known world, it comes as no wonder that today Malta is one of the most densely populated countries in the world, with 440,000 inhabitants over a surface area of approximately 316 square kilometres.

The richness of its fortified cities and their majestic walls, the palaces, gardens and ornately-decorated churches are the envy of many. Prior to the arrival of the Knights of the Sovereign Military Order of St John, in 1530, the Maltese economy was mainly agricultural. Maltese fishermen were also very conservative, never venturing beyond inshore waters. Up to the 16th century, the Feudal Lords had been governing Malta from towering Mdina, '*La Città Vecchia*' nowadays more affectionately referred to as 'The Silent City'. It is very central, being practically equidistant from all the points on the coastline, thus offering refuge and protection to all the islanders from the incessant peril of the Muslim pirate raids.

Valletta **A PERSONAL CITY GUIDE**

The arrival of the Knights, and their maritime forces, meant that the economic activity shifted from Mdina towards the area of the two harbours, where the main city of the time was Vittoriosa, in Grand Harbour. Thirty-five years later, just after the Great Siege, the Knights would construct a new city, henceforth to be known as Valletta, on Mount Sceberras, the peninsula separating the two harbours.

I shall base my account on two views. The first will be the view from the Upper Barrakka gardens of the Grand Harbour towards the south-east. This sheds a light on the socio-economic life of the Maltese people who mingled with their overlords in its glorious and turbulent history, and will lead to. a short description of why Valletta was built and the way its population grew with the port activity and also to its eventual decline. The view from the other side, from the top of the walls of Hastings Gardens and the St Paul's Anglican Cathedral towards Marsamxett Harbour on

VALLETTA AND ITS HARBOURS

The magnificent entrance to the Grand Harbour

the north-west, shows the more recent economic development of creeks and Manoel Island with yacht marinas, hotels and modern residential buildings.

The view from Valletta's Upper Barrakka is one of the most familiar sights on the Island with the numerous deep creeks stretching from the harbour entrance far to the left, through the facing creeks housing Kalkara and the Three Cities, all the way to the inner harbour waters of Marsa on the right.

The **breakwater** at the mouth of Grand Harbour was built by the British in 1903. The harbour was regarded as the advance naval station for the British navy in

The construction of the breakwater, 1903

Valletta A PERSONAL CITY GUIDE

the Mediterranean and the main reason for the construction of this breakwater was that the harbour was exposed to the strong north-eastern Grecian wind, known as the *Grigal*, particularly during the winter months. Another reason was more of a naval strategic nature. The mouth of the harbour was too wide and open, and already then it was considered to be vulnerable to attacks by torpedoes and submarines, the relatively new arrivals to naval warfare. The Germans had already developed the submarine with lethal torpedoes and the British naval strategists sought to protect the naval vessels. This farsightedness would prove its worth in the Second World War when, in July 1941, the breakwater and its defences helped to foil an attack by Italian *maiali* (human torpedoes) and the MT explosive boats (*barchini*) against the British fleet in the harbour. One of these machines, whose pilot had been killed making it possible for it to be recovered intact, is nowadays on display at the National War Museum in Fort Saint Elmo.

Fort Ricasoli on the extreme left of the view, was built in 1680 by a Florentine knight after having been designed by a Flemish engineer, Carlos de Grunenbergh. It was subsequently remodified by Rene de Tigné and Charles de Mondion in 1714. This site has served as the set for a number of films shot in Malta, including the blockbusters *Gladiator* (2000) with Russell Crowe, and *Troy* (2004) with Brad Pitt and Diane Kruger, as well as scenes or episodes from *Julius Caesar* (2002), *Helen of Troy* (2003), *Agora* (2009) and the more recent *Game of Thrones* and *Murder on the Orient Express*. Film making has developed into a strong economic activity. Local actors, carpenters, make-up artists, chauffeurs and crews are engaged by film makers during production, not to count the hundreds of extras used for crowd scenes. Malta has featured in more than 250 films since its historic buildings, landscapes, beaches and deep blue sea provide ideal settings. Malta is dubbed as the mini-Hollywood of the Med. Come and explore the numerous places and settings.

On the headland to the right of Ricasoli, having crossed over through Rinella Bay, we see **Bighi Hospital** with its imposing neo-classical portico and Grecian Doric colonnades. This building was designed by Whitmore and built in 1830. Facing Bighi Hospital on the Valletta side of the harbour, is the *Sacra Infermeria* (nowadays the Mediterranean Conference Centre) which was built much earlier, in 1574, by the Knights, who were a hospitaller order. In fact, their eight-pointed cross (the Maltese cross) still features

The Saluting Battery below the Upper Barrakka

in the emblem of health support organisations such as the Saint John's Ambulance Brigade. The presence of these hospitals, no longer used as such, meant that the Maltese have participated in another economic activity, providing medical and nursing work, since the time of the Knights (1530-1798) and the British (1800-1979). Maltese doctors, like Mikielanġ Grima, were employed by the Grand Master of the Order himself, and by the Head of the French Langue to work with French surgeons and physicians. Even under British Rule, a few Maltese doctors were enrolled in the British Army side-by-side with British medical staff in the Garrison Hospital within the *Sacra Infermeria*, in Cottonera Hospital (today St Edward's College), in David Bruce Military Hospital, Mtarfa and also in King George V Merchant Seamen's Hospital (today Sir Paul Boffa Hospital, Floriana). Dr Temi Zammit was one such doctor who worked with the namesake of the Mtarfa Hospital, David Bruce, in a joint medical research project. After having graduated in medicine from the University of Malta, Zammit specialised in bacteriology in London and Paris. In 1905 he discovered that contaminated milk was the vector for transmission from the blood of goats to humans of the bacterium causing undulant, or Mediterranean, fever. The disease would be named after his British medical collaborator – *Brucellosis Melitensis* – and their discovery, and the elimination of the bacterium by pasteurisation of milk, greatly contributed to the elimination from the Islands of this disease. Zammit's work earned him a knighthood from the British Crown, making him Sir Temi Zammit. During WWII, penicillin which was then still a closely-guarded secret and still in its early days, was used in trials, very effectively too, on Maltese patients. Nowadays, Maltese doctors obtain their first degree at the University of Malta and then many specialise, mostly in the United Kingdom in leading consultancy centres. Malta has always benefited from, and contributed to the latest medical technologies and knowhow of its rulers. The Maltese were exposed to the current latest prevention and intervention methodologies. Free medical care is part of the country's social welfare policy, and top notch hospital facilities, including a state-of-the-art EU-financed oncology centre, are offered through the new Mater Dei Hospital.

Fort St Angelo (*Castrum Maris*), next headland to the right of Bighi, was used by the Aragonese in the 13th century. This old sea-facing castle was in a very bad state of repair when Grand Master l'Isle Adam came to Malta as the head of the Knights, and made it his residence in 1530. This is the only castle or fortress in Malta which has an actual sea-moat. Attached to it, by a bridge over this moat, we have the suburb of Vittoriosa, known as *Birgu*. This town started to come to life when the Knights established a temporary residence to repair their galleys in the winter months in the safe calm waters in the Dockyard (Galley's) creek between the Vittoriosa and Senglea promontories. This led to the tremendous expansion of job opportunities in and around the harbour. By 1750, five towns had established themselves as a result – Vittoriosa (*Birgu*), Cospicua (*Bormla*), Senglea (*Isla*) are collectively known as Cottonera, while on the facing side we have Floriana and Valletta. Together these five towns contained

Fort St Angelo

about half of the population of the Islands. The occasional oil painting can help to evoke the images of magnificent sailing ships entering or leaving the harbour amongst which the centipede-like galleys of the Order of St John, with hundreds of rowers, being slaves, galley convicts or volunteers. The Knights policed them wearing their colourful uniforms. The Maritime Museum, situated on the waterfront in Birgu, is housed in the building which used to serve as the British naval bakery. Between the 19th and 21st centuries, boatmen ferried British naval commanders, officers and all other hands from the naval vessels to shore and back using the traditional Maltese *dgħajsa,* a gondola-like boat particular to Grand Harbour. There were hundreds of such boatmen, plying to and fro all along the harbour, offering passage to sailors in possession of a shore leave pass, hence earning the boat the nickname of *dgħajsa tal-pass.* This boat was widely-used by the thousands and thousands of sailors who passed through Grand Harbour over the many years of British occupation. It is no wonder then that its name eventually entered the British lexicon, and is to be found in the Oxford English Dictionary to describe this particular type of boat found only in the Maltese Grand Harbour.

Senglea, the next promontory to the right of Birgu, and its drydocks were important economic pillars for the Maltese working population. Who, if not the largest imperial power and the owner of the largest mercantile and naval fleets – Great Britain, could have exploited to the maximum, the potential offered by one of the largest natural harbours in the Mediterranean? It became the busiest port in the Mediterranean. Seven dry docks were built around Senglea. After the opening of the Suez Canal in 1869, if India was the jewel of the British empire, Malta, with Valletta and its harbour were its diamond. Paradoxically, Malta flourished when there were wars, namely in 1827 when the alliance of France, Russia and Britain fought the Turco-Egyptian fleet, in 1853 during the Crimean War, and during World War I. In contrast, **t**imes of peace meant a slowdown in economic activity, resulting in mass unemployment, poverty and hunger**.** In times of war, Maltese workers plugged their tobacco pipes with gold sovereigns. During the Crimean War, money was circulated in profusion, and every tradesman was busy, morning, noon and night. Saddlers, tin men, outfitters, tailors, shoemakers and cutters all charged rates matching those of London's West End. The peaceful slump of the aftermath of WW1, on the other hand, meant that in 1920 some 4,500 workers, representing 2% of the population, had to emigrate to North Africa, Southern France and the Adriatic. The Grand Harbour was no longer the busiest port in the Mediterranean, not only because of the reduction of imperial expenditure, but because larger ships were now bypassing Malta.

The **Malta Drydocks** were run by the British up to mid-20th century, and after a few failed privatisation experiences, it was turned to a public enterprise run by the workers themselves. Still functioning at great loss, the drydocks had become disguised unemployment and were unproductive, and a burden on public coffers, leading to their final closure in 2010. However, the technical skills learnt by these workers led to their immediate re-

Senglea and the Malta Drydocks

Valletta A PERSONAL CITY GUIDE

employment in the maintenance of civil aircraft operating from Malta, and in other industrial sectors. The drydocks themselves were taken over, albeit on a smaller scale, by the Neapolitan company, Palumbo, which also absorbed back some of the workers previously working there.

Nowadays, **Grand Harbour** has once again become a web of activity due to the hustle and bustle generated by cruise lining. New berth facilities can take as many as seven huge cruise liners concurrently. These massive hotel-like ships annually disgorge over 600,000 visitors on to shore, a bonanza for taxi drivers, day tour operators and owners of *karozzini* (the Maltese traditional horse-drawn cabs). The waterfront cafes and restaurants in the cruise liner terminal are also leading culinary destinations in their own right, offering all types of fare from typically Mediterranean, to American-influenced and even oriental cuisines.

We have been looking at the side facing **Valletta**. But, what about Valletta itself? It was founded on 28 March 1566, because the Order of St John were fearing another attack from Suleiman the Magnificent after

Upper Barrakka and the lift

having failed to take over the Islands in the Great Siege of 1565. The City was designed and planned by the Italian architect Francesco Laparelli, and built by the Maltese architect Ġirolmu Cassar. It was financed by the kingdoms of France, Portugal, Spain and by the Vatican, through Pope Pius V. It was constructed on the barren peninsula known as Mount Sceberras. Its features include high and magnificent bastions, streets organised in a grid, and Fort St Elmo at its tip. It was the intention of the Order to build their palaces, auberges, cathedral and hospital there, and to make Valletta their permanent home. Between 1566 and 1571 this led to a massive construction of the whole city from scratch, with the many high buildings seen, being invisibly mirrored underground. Besides water storage there are rail tunnels, foot passages, as well as bomb shelters used between 1940-1943 to protect civilians from Axis air raids. Malta was the most intensely bombarded place during the Second World War, and Valletta and the facing three cities of Cottonera suffered heavy damages and casualties. Following this destruction, over the past fifty years, the urban inner harbour area has sprawled and more than doubled in size, making construction one of the main drivers of the economy.

In 1667, Valletta had 1,891 residences and a population of 10,744. In 1830 there were 4,326 residences housing 21,341 people, reaching a maximum of 24,450 in 1930. There was much activity with the toing and froing of harbour boats between ship and shore. The streets of Valletta with the wharf-side bars came to life. With the constant use of the Upper Barrakka lift, many a soldier and sailor remembers the red-light district known as 'The Gut' in Strait Street, another very particular economic activity. Old photos show streets lined with shops, wine and snack bars, tearooms, tobacconists, bakeries and sundry. After 1970, Valletta's population of 15,500, started dropping drastically to a mere 5,680 residents today, with the daytime working population being however much higher, with lawyers, civil servants, businessmen, shoppers and tourists flocking to the city in droves. Nightlife activities had shifted towards to the new entertainment area of St Julian's

Valletta A PERSONAL CITY GUIDE

but in recent years in Valletta a new activity connected with calmer dining, and theatrical and other cultural activities is slowly growing.

We go now to the other side, and from one of the bastions between Hastings Garden and the Anglican Cathedral we savour the view over **Marsamxett Harbour** on the north-west flank. On the right, at the entrance of the harbour on the other side, we see Tigné Point, then Sliema creek further in. Just opposite us we can see **Manoel Island**, a real island in the middle of the harbour. Its isolation, though being surrounded by water, made it ideal to be used as the *lazaretto*, an Italian word denoting a quarantine station for maritime travellers. Its magnificent buildings have recently been restored and there are plans for their use as a conference and events centre. Surrounding Manoel Island mainly to its left, we see Ta' Xbiex, with its lovely waterfront stately buildings being complemented by a long yacht marina which stretches all the way from Manoel Island, to Msida and Sa Maison. These last two towns previously housed military activity in the form of submarine bases, and the torpedo depot. This harbour now boasts the largest yacht and pleasure boat aggregation on the Islands, as well as the Tigné Point luxurious apartment blocks.

The economic activity surrounding Valletta has gone full circle. There is a stark contrast to, and far-removal from the old fortress economy dependent on military, particularly naval expenditure especially on war. From an economy driven by conflict and the suffering it generates, the harbours straddling Valletta have now moved on to activity which is more pleasant and directly linked to the finer aspects of life - business, leisure, gastronomy, travel and real estate. In 2004, Malta joined the European Union and adopted the Euro in 2008. Access to EU structural funds and cohesion policy have meant massive investment in conservation and restoration works on the exterior and interior of buildings in and around Valletta. No longer can you see shrubs on the bastion walls in between the limestone bricks and most buildings were scraped clean and restored to their former glory and original colour. Tourists remain awestruck with the sheer magnificence and beauty of the Maltese hybrid of Medieval, Baroque, Neo-classical and British architecture found in Valletta.

Valletta has nowadays become intrinsically linked with its harbours and their waterfronts since, in recent years, links between the City and its facing shores have been re-established. Using the old boating routes, scheduled water-borne transport using modern ferries, are available in both harbours making the Sliema – Valletta – Cottonera link possible in a very short transit time. What could be more pleasant than breakfast in Sliema, followed by shopping, sight-seeing and lunch in Valletta, then a walk around the three cities of Cottonera, followed by a quiet dinner at one of the waterfront restaurants in Birgu. Then back to the Sliema side for some more vigorous night activity. All with a smile …

References:
Malta from Colonial Dependency to Economic Viability (Dr Edward J Spiteri)
Trade and Port Activity in Malta 1750 – 1800 (John Debono)
Richard Ellis – The photography collection - Grand harbour and Cottonera (Natalino Fenech)
Bliet u Rhula Maltin (Alfie Guillaumier)
Malta – The Baroque Island (Conrad Thake and Quentin Hughes)
Malta – War & Peace an Architectural Chronicle 1800-2000 (Conrad Thake and Quentin Hughes)

Valletta A PERSONAL CITY GUIDE

Sciortino's Monument of Christ the King